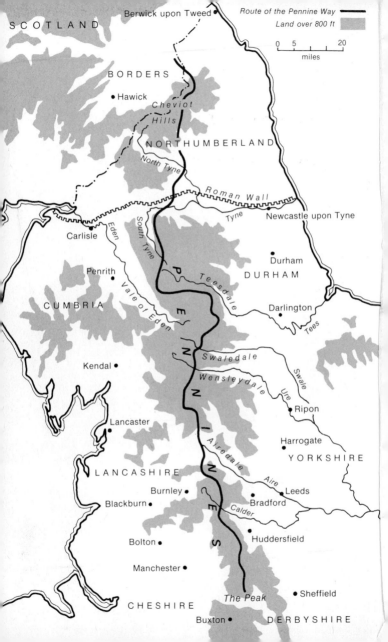

A guide to the Pennine Way

Also by Christopher John Wright
A guide to the Pilgrims' Way (1971)
A guide to Offa's Dyke Path (1975)

A guide to
the Pennine Way

Christopher John Wright

Constable London

Published by Constable & Co Ltd
10 Orange Street London WC2H 7EG
© 1967 Christopher John Wright
First published 1967
Reprinted 1968
2nd edition 1975
3rd edition 1979
Reprinted 1981

ISBN 0 09 462760 6

Set in Monophoto Times New Roman 9pt
Printed in Great Britain by
BAS Printers Limited, Over Wallop, Hampshire

Contents

Contents

Among the projects designed to extend walking facilities in the National Parks was the promotion of the first long-distance route called the Pennine Way, which runs northwards from the Peak in Derbyshire along the moorland spine of northern England as far as the Scottish Border, a total distance of 250 miles/402 km.

The idea of this continuous footpath was first suggested in 1935 by Tom Stephenson, journalist and rambler, and was largely inspired by the affinity to the Pilgrim's Way and by the Appalachian Trail and the famous John Muir Trail in the U.S.A.

The project quickly gained support, especially among the rambler's and other open-air organisations, and at a conference held in 1938 representatives unanimously agreed that a Pennine Way was desirable, and that 'the wide, health-giving moorlands and high places of solitude, the features of natural beauty and the places of historical interest along the Pennine Way give this route a special character and attractiveness which should be available for all time as a natural heritage of the youth of the country, and of all who feel the call of the hills and lonely places.' This footpath, it was emphasised, should be nothing more than a way trodden by walkers. Any artificially surfaced track would be as objectionable as a metalled road.

Before the War, members of the Ramblers' Association and the Youth Hostels Association had surveyed the 250 miles/402 km of the proposed route. The results of this survey, which revealed that 90 miles/145 km of new footpaths were needed, were supplied to the National Parks Commission (now renamed the Countryside Commission), who have the responsibility for preparing and submitting to the Secretary of State, Department of the Environment, proposals for the establishment of long-distance routes.

In due course provision was made by the Commission for the development of the Pennine Way as the first of the long-distance paths which may be established under the National Parks and Access to the Countryside Act, 1949, and, after consulting the local authorities concerned, they submitted a report to the Minister for his approval in June, 1951.

On 16th July, 1951, official approval for the Pennine Way was granted by Mr. Hugh Dalton. The Minister's sanction having been given, the highway authorities were required by the Act to open up the new paths which were needed to complete the route.

On 24th April, 1965, the Right Hon. F. T. Willey, M.P., Minister of Land and Natural Resources, officially opened the Pennine Way at an informal ceremony at Malham. The National Parks Commission was responsible for the event and its chairman, Lord Strang, G.C.B., G.C.M.G., M.B.E., and Tom Stephenson for the Ramblers' Association were the speakers. The 200 invited guests—representatives of all the bodies who have put so much work into bringing the scheme into fruition—were supported by a 2,000 strong band of walkers who could not be included in the list of formal invitations.

By using existing paths and old half-forgotten tracks wherever possible, the route is now complete. New paths will only be rough tracks, and constructional work will be limited to the provision of stiles and a few footbridges, occasional signposting in the villages and at the crossing of roadways, and the erection of cairns or stakes on high ground. These latter will never be sufficiently numerous to prevent the use of map and compass in the many places where paths are non-existent.

Accommodation
Facilities for overnight accommodation and refreshment at suitable intervals along the Pennine Way route have been improved over recent years, notably by the addition of new youth hostels and bed-and-breakfast lodgings. The county councils are empowered by the National Parks Act to arrange for the provision, whether by themselves or other persons, of accommodation, meals and refreshment, and although this is an on-going long-term policy no difficulties should now be met in the search for suitable lodgings on the route.

There are twenty-one Youth Hostels on or near the Pennine Way, but recognised camp sites are scattered, many being unduly exposed. Accommodation can also be found in many farmhouses, but it should be sought in advance. Few farms make a practice of catering for visitors and it is unfair to expect to be provided with food and lodging, especially during June, July and August, the hill-farmers' busiest months.

For details of accommodation on the Pennine Way route consult the Y.H.A. Handbook, the Rambler's Association Bed and Breakfast Guide, the Cyclists' Touring Club Handbook and the Camping Club of Great Britain Sites List, all of which are reliable in every way. The Pennine Way Council, a consortium of local authorities and organisations having an interest in the Pennine Way, have published an accommodation list. It cannot claim to be comprehensive, but it is published regularly (no address given). It can be obtained from information centres and youth hostels along the route.

Route finding

The Pennine Way provides some of the roughest walking to be found in Britain, but in good weather it is within the capacity of anyone able to undertake 12–15 miles/19–24 km of hill-walking a day, sometimes across boggy ground or through expanses of heather and moor grass. In rain, mist, snow or high winds it can prove arduous and even exhausting for the hardiest walkers, and should certainly not be attempted in such conditions by anyone unable to steer a course by map and compass.

Tens of thousands of walkers have now 'done' the Pennine Way . Their feet have worn deep grooves in it and occasionally in the patience of farmers whose land it crosses. It varies from the Indian-file track crossing pastures (where it is least defined) to an extended quagmire several feet wide on the peaty moorland. It has been reinforced in places with stretches of plastic carpet and steps up steep slopes. It is well but not always obviously marked. The official 'Pennine Way' directional signs are usually found in places where they are really least needed and hardly ever where they would be most appreciated. It is to be hoped that this guide book gives a more useful and detailed assistance in clearly defining the official route on the map, though more way-marking is required on the ground.

The occasional directional signs and cairns should be supplemented in some more systematic manner, perhaps by coloured symbols as on the Continent and in our own Forest Parks. Such a system would be most useful especially at complex stretches, such as Brontëland, Wark Forest and the Border Fence, while being quite unnecessary for such places as Hadrian's Wall, Teesdale and the River Aire.

Some methods of waymarking would arouse considerable opposition—cairns built on Kinder Scout have been dismantled repeatedly—but a successful, cheap and easy method could not possibly disfigure the countryside or destroy the essential wilderness of the moors.

The Countryside Commission have erected some two dozen notice boards—about 8 ft/2·4 m high and 3 ft/0·9 m wide—at various points throughout the route, showing local sections of 1:25,000 scale maps, laminated in plastic, giving brief advice about equipment and the Country Code. These maps are situated at the following places:

1 Edale—at the start of the Pennine Way.
2 Crowden—outside the Pennine Way hostel.
3 Standedge—opposite the Floating Light PH.
4 Blackstone Edge—on A58 at The White House PH.
5 Ponden—on road at W end of reservoir.
6 Lothersdale—at farm next to Hare & Hounds PH.
7 Gargrave—on car park beside bridge over R. Aire.
8 Malham—beside public toilets next to Buck Inn.
9 Horton in Ribblesdale—on car park near public toilets near The Crown PH.
10 Hawes—in main street, near car park and public toilets.
11 Thwaite—in village street, next to telephone call box.
12 Bowes—at A66/A67 road junction.
13 Middleton in Teesdale—in main street, next to public toilets.
14 Teesdale—at Widdybank Farm.
15 Dufton—on village green.
16 Garrigill—by church gates, near George & Dragon PH.
17 Slaggyford—in centre of village.
18 Greenhead—in lay-by on A69 E of Gap Shields.

19 Hadrians Wall—at Steel Rigg car park and public toilets N of Once Brewed.

20 Bellingham—in village street on car park next to public toilets.

21 Lords Shaw—at cattle grid on road N of Lords Shaw.

22 Byrness—on The Raw picnic site.

23 Windy Gyle.

24 Kirk Yetholm—on village green.

The Pennine Way walker will require a compass and the following 1:50,000 scale maps:

74 Kelso
80 The Cheviot Hills
86 Haltwhistle & Bewcastle
91 Appleby
92 Barnard Castle & Richmond
98 Wensleydale & Wharfedale
103 Blackburn & Burnley
109 Manchester
110 Sheffield & Huddersfield

The maps in this book are at a scale of approximately one half inch to one mile. The official route, and the official alternatives for bad weather, are marked by a broken line.

Since this book was first published in August 1967 there have been many other Pennine Way 'guidebooks' published. Whilst only one or two can be called true walkers' guides, a complete list is given in the bibliography on p. 229, and readers will be able to compare the relative merits of each.

1 Be properly clad
Wear strong boots and adequate windproof clothing. Carry spare
woollens and a waterproof. Even in summer it can be cold on a
mountain top.

2 Carry essential equipment
Always carry a compass and a 1:50,000 map, or better, a
1:25,000 map of the district, and be certain that with their aid
you can steer a safe course in mist or darkness. Carry also a
whistle and an electric torch (with spare bulb and battery). Carry
energy giving food—such as chocolate, glucose and dried fruits.

3 Allow yourself ample time
The moors and fells are vast and should be treated with respect.
Winter days are short, and even in summer bad weather may
delay your progress. Add to a normal walking time of one hour
for 3 miles/4·8 km, one hour for each 1,500 ft/457 m of ascent.
Following the Pennine Way from Edale to Kirk Yetholm
involves climbing approximately 32,000 ft/9 754 m in addition to
250 miles/402 km measured from the map. In a publicity leaflet
the Countryside Commission states: 'Bearing in mind that the
frequent changes in direction and level of the path make straight
line map reading unrealistic, an allowance of about 25% should
be added to get a truer idea of the distances involved.'

4 Say where you are going
Before you set out in the morning, leave word of your intended
route and destination. Search parties like to know at least in
which direction to start.

5 Watch the weather
Clouds often form quickly on mountain tops, so be sure of your
bearing before landmarks are hidden in mist.

6 Safety in numbers

Think twice before going on the hills alone. There should be at least three in a party, for if an accident occurs one can stay with the patient while the third seeks help.

7 Distress signal

In an emergency, give the recognised distress signal of six blasts on a whistle or six flashes of a torch in one minute, followed by a minute's silence, repeated as necessary. The answering signal is three blasts or flashes in a minute, followed by a minute's silence and then repeated.

The Countryside Commission have prepared the Country Code as a guide to visitors, some of whom are perhaps unaccustomed to country ways. Please remember and observe the following standards of good manners when you go to enjoy the beauties and the pleasures of the garden that is Britain's countryside.

1 **Guard against all risks of fire**

2 **Fasten all gates**

3 **Keep dogs under proper control**

4 **Keep to the paths across farm land**

5 **Avoid damaging fences, hedges and walls**

6 **Leave no litter**

7 **Safeguard water supplies**

8 **Protect wild life, plants and trees**

9 **Go carefully on country roads**

10 **Respect the life of the countryside**

Edale to Crowden

Edale

The Pennine Way begins at the top of Edale village, a secluded
little place with pretty houses and lovely gardens, but also
perhaps the most popular walking centre in the Peak District
National Park. The Peak District Warden Service is based in
Edale, where there is also a mountain rescue post and a National
Park Information Centre with an excellent camp site adjoining. A
Youth Hostel is situated some 2 miles/3 km away to the east at
Lady Booth Brook. Other accommodation is available at the
Church Hotel and at Armfield, Upper Booth, while Cooper's
Cafe at the head of the village provides refreshments.

Kinder Scout

Immediately north of the village is Kinder Scout, an extremely
irregular plateau covered with peat bog and extending over 15 sq.
miles/39 sq. km. The sides of the plateau are steep and sometimes
precipitous, and the streams have cut deep cloughs where
sparkling water runs over moss-green boulders, cascading down
into innumerable golden pools, with the coarse silver-green
moorland grass on either hand. The plateau summit is covered
with many large muddy hollows, called 'groughs,' made by the
action of water on the spongy soil. Groughs vary in depth from a
few feet/metres to 15 ft/4·5 m and more; some are narrow
enough to jump and others more than 20 ft/6 m wide. On the
map it looks easy, but at all times Kinder presents interesting
problems of navigation.

Grindsbrook: the start of the Pennine Way

The southern end of the 250 mile/402 m long Pennine Way is
reached by passing northwards through Edale village to the road
head and the log bridge over Grindsbrook. A well-defined path
leads through the Meadows and a mixed copse to a stile and the
crossing of Golden Clough and the wild hollow of Grindsbrook,
the most striking of all watercourses on Kinder Scout. As we

The start of the Pennine Way. The log bridge spans Grindsbrook above Edale Village

climb by the wide brown track we can study the geology of
Kinder as the valley sides close in.

The plateau of Kinder is formed by a slab of millstone grit,
several hundred feet/metres thick, resting on a pedestal of shale.
The well-drained shale slopes are littered with landslips and
transported rock debris, with heather, bracken and bilberry
occurring on the fertile soil. The gritstone is rich in potash and
iron, and the soluble material is readily washed out of the porous
rock. The steep rugged gritstone cliffs are black from grime and
weathering, but the natural colour of this rough granular stone
varies from faint gold to brown.

In a little over 1·5 miles/2·4 km from Edale the main stream
turns to the north (right), but we continue up the confusing
tributary north-west to Fox Holes and the edge of the summit
plateau.

Kinder Scout
The unusual terrain of the gritstone moor is now revealed;
rolling contours of bilberry, crowberry and acid-loving grasses.
Kinder and Bleaklow receive a mean annual rainfall of 63 inches/
160 cm, an ideal climate for the Cotton Grass sedge, the main
plant cover on these high peat moors. The moors are wild and
desolate for much of the year but are strikingly transferred by the
white mass of Cotton Grass in June and July.

The moors are the haunt of grouse and curlew, but more
widespread is the meadow pipit, a small brown bird which is
identified by the white side feathers of the tail as it rises from the
ground.

Grouse chuckle and cluck among the peat hags and shout
'Goback!' when disturbed. Here you are an immeasurable
distance from everywhere, surrounded by sky and black peat.
The track is barely distinguished between the tawny grass as we
continue in the direction to join the feeder of Crowden Brook,
which we follow slightly west of north towards Crowden Head,
2,070 ft/631 m.

The peaty wastes are crossed northwest to join the head streams
of the River Kinder, which leads north then west to the

Grindslow Knoll   Upper Tor   Nether Tor

The Nab

Grindsbrook

To Sheffield ▶

◀ To Manchester

Kinder Scout and Edale under snow, from Mam Tor Great Ridge

Grindsbrook from Ringing Roger

Fox Holes

2062´

Anvil Stone

Grindslow Knoll

Ringing Roger

Peat 'groughs' on Kinder Scout

Downfall, 3 miles/5 km from Edale. The river flows between some of the deepest groughs on Kinder and the stream bed is flecked with shining white pebbles in silvery sand. The river widens at Kinder Gates, a dramatic gritstone gateway, and the path is then clear to the Downfall, crossing and recrossing the shallow stream as it meanders.

If the clouds are low when you have reached the top of Grindsbrook, a compass bearing of 290 degrees will bring you out at the head of the Downfall. If the weather is really bad, it will be best to avoid the featureless tops and take the alternative route via Upper Booth and Edale Cross.

Alternative Route over Kinder 4·5 miles/7·24 km
Edale to Downfall via Edale Cross
From the road head at the Nags Head in Edale village take the path that leads westwards through a gateway, and follow a stream bed that emerges in the pastures below Grindslow Knoll. (An alternative way to Grindsbrook diverges here, crossing the hillside diagonally northwards to the Sledge Road and the summit of Grindslow Knoll, and the plateau edge to the head of Grindsbrook.) A well-defined path leads below Broad Lee Bank Tor to the hamlet of Upper Booth and the crossing of Crowden Brook by a tiny one arch bridge.

A good track now follows the course of the River Noe, and in less than 1·5 miles/2·4 km the packhorse bridge below Jacob's Ladder is reached. This is on the route of the old packhorse track which crossed the moors between Edale and Hayfield.

Jacob's Ladder rises opposite, a steep track scarring the almost vertical hillside. It was so named because it was first opened up by one Jacob Marshall, who used to send his laden donkey by the easier winding route while he himself went straight up.

The true path leads to the right and not up the boulder strewn scree directly in front. It is easier to climb the slope by taking the donkey track to the left past the ruins of Edale Head House. Thirty years ago this farm was standing intact, though empty, and its walls provide the last shelter before crossing Kinder.

On again to Edale Cross at 1,750 ft/533 m, where on the right-

The River Kinder at Kinder Gates

hand side of the track stands a rudely shaped and badly mutilated cross. This medieval stone was probably erected by Cistercian monks to mark the packhorse route.

We now leave this track and turn right through the gateway by the cross, and take the peaty slopes up to the triangulation station on Kinderlow, at 2,077 ft/633 m. Now continue northwards by a path along the western edge, crossing Red Brook and joining the main Pennine Way route by the Shelter Stone above Kinder Downfall.

Main Route:
Downfall to Snake Pass 4 miles/6·4 km
Kinder Downfall is a fine sight in wet weather when the River Kinder plunges over the precipice. The Downfall is where a great triangular wedge has been hacked out of the western escarpment, and when the river thunders over in full spate the wind is said to blow the spray so high that it can be seen in Stockport, 10 miles/ 16 km away. The foreground, as you look down 500 ft/152 m or more, is magnificent, and so is the view on a clear day. On the far hillside is the little Mermaid Pool, with the usual legend of the mermaid visiting the pool on Easter Eve, and the sure immortality awaiting him who sees her bathing.

From the head of the Downfall descend along the northern edge north-westerly to Mill Hill, crossing the head of William Clough, then north-easterly on the watershed over Moss Castle passing Featherbed Top to reach the Snake Road at its highest point, 1,680 ft/512 m.

The Snake Road was built in 1820, just before people began to see that the steam engine would inevitably supersede the horse-drawn coach. A Turnpike Act of 1818 sanctioned the building of this road so that Sheffield and Manchester could be more directly linked. The road and pass is so named because the moors hereabouts have been owned by the Cavendish family for a long period, and the snake features prominently in that family's coat of arms.

Kinder Downfall

Snake Pass to Bleaklow 4 miles/6·4 km

From Snake Pass to Doctor's Gate near Old Woman the land is
so worn and saturated that the Pennine Way has been diverted
along a 0·25 mile/400 m causeway of plastic webbing laid on rafts
of brushwood which squelches at every step.

Doctor's Gate is the paved section of a Roman Road which
connected forts at Hope and Glossop. It was the only route
across the tops before the turnpike road, and is between three
and four feet wide. Doctor's Gate may have some connection
with William Senior's plans in Chatsworth, where it is referred to
as 'Doctor Talbot's Gate' and Camden used the modern form of
'Doctor's Gate' in 1789.

Continuing forward by occasional boundary stakes we go
along Devil's Dike, and round the head of Crooked Clough
passing Higher Shelf Stones. Less than 100 yds/91 m to the
north-east of Higher Shelf Stones summit a USAF Super
Fortress crashed during the Berlin Air Lift in 1948. The torn and
twisted remains have long since been removed by souvenir-
hunters and national park litter wardens.

But we must press on, for Bleaklow is probably harder going
than even Kinder. Pass over Shelf Moss and Wain Stones to
Bleaklow Head, 2,060 ft/628 m, 10 miles/16 km from Edale.

Walking across Bleaklow takes you where the great silence of
the moors are broken only by the cries of moor-haunting birds—
the red grouse, the lovely call of the curlew, the plaintive cries of
the lapwing, and the liquid notes of the golden plover.

Public access to the moorland areas of Kinder, Bleaklow,
Langsett, Longdendale and Chew will be restricted on some days
in the grouse shooting season, 12th August to 10th December.
Arrangements have been made with the landowners by the Peak
Park Planning Board for shooting to be confined to limited areas
on any one day, thus leaving a greater part of the area
accessible. Please consult notice boards and avoid those areas
where shooting is due to take place.

Grouse shooting and sheep are part of the scene and part of
the economy of the countryside, but in recent years the relative
value of sheep grazing as against grouse shooting has materially
changed.

Plastic carpet at the Snake Pass

On Sheep

Sheep are of greatest importance, and these hill and moorland areas are used primarily for sheep grazing. The Derbyshire Gritstone breed predominates. It can readily be recognised, having a black and white speckled face and legs, grey fleece and no horns. The Swaledale is smaller than the Gritstone, but has horns, black face and greyish nose. Next in number are the Scotch Blackface—a horned sheep with distinctive black face—and Lonk, which resembles Gritstone in many ways but is slightly larger and has horns. The Whitefaced Woodland, a white-faced, horned sheep, is somewhat rarer.

On the lower ground heavier breeds are kept, such as the Kerry Hill, Cluns and Hampshires. These sheep need better food and kinder weather, and are much more dependent on supplementary feeding than are the hill breeds.

Bleaklow to Longdendale 3 miles/5 km

From Bleaklow Head descend due north to the head of Wildboar Grain then westerly to John Track Well and Torside Clough, and from the confluence of two streams climb on to the mound of Torside Castle. Take a course east and north of the Castle over the top of Clough Edge, and then take the footpath down to Reaps in Longdendale. There were proposals for an additional Trans-Pennine Motorway to the M62 that would run through Longdendale to connect Manchester with Sheffield, but it has been shelved. It had been argued that as the valley had already been scarred by road, rail, electricity and reservoirs a new motorway would have made very little difference. The desirability and need for such a road was questioned, and as the route passed through a National Park the proposal raised much opposition.

Longdendale

A track leads to the Glossop road, route B6105, where cross over the railway and take the track over the dam at the foot of Torside Reservoir, and path to route A628, the Sheffield-Manchester trunk road.

From the road take a footpath north to Highstones Farm,

Hey Edge

Hostel

Bareholme Moss

B6105

Crowden-in-Longdendale

where you can refresh yourself at a delicious spring which issues near an old barn, and descend to Crowden Brook and the new hostel (2 miles/3·2 km from Reaps, 15 miles/24 km from Edale).

The new hostel at Crowden was opened on 4th June, 1965, by Mr. Willey, Minister of Land and Natural Resources. The hostel has been converted from six cottages, but visitors do not have to be Y.H.A. members to stay overnight, or use the cafe which is open daily. The hostel was built on the initiative of the Peak Park Planning Board, with an Exchequer grant, a lease from Manchester Corporation, and the whole is managed by the Youth Hostels Association.

It has been a strenuous day's walk to reach Crowden, the first place of accommodation since leaving Edale. The next stage, as well as providing not quite such hard going, also involves shorter distances if accommodation is sought at a youth hostel. A new hostel has now been firmly established at Marsden, and this cuts down the distances to 10 miles/16 km from Crowden and 15 miles/24 km from Mankinholes. Other suitable lodgings are, however, harder to find.

Crowden to Standedge

Longdendale

Longdendale is an important valley carrying communications
between Manchester and Sheffield. It lies in Cheshire, the reason
being that the Earls of Chester laid claim to this 'corridor' route
to avoid having to pay the toll on salt which would have been
claimed had Longdendale belonged to Derbyshire or Lancashire.
One of the salt routes from Cheshire's brine pits followed
Longdendale into Yorkshire, and it was made a turnpike road in
1731.

In 1848 the Etherow was dammed up to form the present chain
of reservoirs to serve Manchester with water. Completed in 1862
they now have a total capacity of 3,000 million gallons/13 638
million litres. The flanks of Longdendale are jealously guarded
by the North West Water Authority. The purity of supply is
protected by restriction, and soil treatments, ploughing and cattle
grazing are prohibited.

Crowden to Black Hill 5 miles/8 km

The Pennine Way after leaving Crowden follows its original line
above Laddow Rocks, and not by Hey Edge and Westend Moss
as shown on some maps.

Retrace your steps along the lane past the hostel, turning left to
the crossing of Crowden Great Brook. Pass through the gate and
after a short distance along the track bear north along the line
marking the western boundary of a firing range. The footpath
rises gradually towards the cliffs on the skyline, and when the
edge of the moor is reached bear right and continue along the
crest of the outcrop to the end, where descend a steep gully to the
base of the cliffs. This is a favourite gritstone outcrop for the
rock climber, and a cave at the base of the cliffs provides shelter
in bad weather.

From Laddow Rocks continue in a northerly direction
contouring round above Crowden Great Brook, then bear north-
easterly over Dun Hill to its source on Black Hill, 1,908 ft/582 m.

Here Holme Moss B.B.C. radio and television transmitter comes into view to the south-east. The 750 ft/228 m mast was built in 1950 and it is visible from a great distance.

To reach Black Hill we have had to cross Soldier's Lump, a vast peat moss, windswept and lifeless. The name is derived from the bench mark used by the men of the Ordnance Survey when they were mapping the area in 1936, although local tradition has it that soldiers were stationed there during the Luddite Riots of 1811–16 (which seems most improbable). The soldiers had unpleasant memories of their work on the 'prodigious muck heap', for the peaty ground would not hold their tent pegs, and several times their only shelter was whirled away into the mists.

Away to the east is the road to Huddersfield, where once stood a famous old coaching inn called 'Bill' o' Jacks'. Here in 1832, William Bradbury, commonly known as Bill o' Jacks, aged 85 years, and his son Thomas, were found one morning dead on the parlour floor. Suspicion alighted on two poachers, also named Bradbury, who were open enemies of the murdered men. William and Thomas Bradbury were gamekeepers as well as innkeepers, and were due to give evidence against the poachers at Pontefract Assizes. The mystery was never solved, the two poachers being acquitted by an English court of law, which should remove all doubt.

Alternative Route:
Black Hill to Standedge 6·5 miles/10·45 km
Black Hill and White Moss are not for the faint-hearted, and in bad weather it is advisable to descend north-east from Black Hill down the head of Hey Clough. After a while a boundary ditch is reached on the left, and this is followed in a straight line to the road A635 a few yards/metres west of the demolished Isle of Skye Inn.

The famous Isle of Skye Inn stood on Wessenden Head near the Meltham road junction, and has saved the life of more than one benighted rambler. Like the equally famous Bill o' Jacks it has been pulled down, under pretence of still 'purer' water. Some of us would have preferred to take our chances with the water as it was and preserve the inns, but the reservoir-makers would not hear of it. One after another these old inns, which have done good service for scores of years, are being pulled down on the grounds of 'pollution' and soon it will be hard to find an inn anywhere near a catchment area.

Chesterton's 'Noah' didn't care where the water went so long as it didn't get into the wine, but the Manchester Corporation didn't care where the beer went so long as it didn't get into the water!

This alternative route crosses the road by the Isle of Skye Inn and strikes north-east to a track from the Meltham road. This track is followed down the Wessenden valley and its series of reservoirs, but 0·3 mile/0·48 km below Wessenden Reservoir it crosses the stream by a footbridge. The route follows the stream westerly round the north side of Black Moss and joins the main route at the south-east corner of the farthest reservoir.

Main Route:
Black Hill to Standedge 5 miles/8 km
From Black Hill the Pennine Way route continues north-west over Wessenden Head Moor via height 1,622 ft/507 m to the road crossing near the 20th milestone on the Greenfield-Holmfirth road A635. It was near here that the bodies of murdered children were discovered early in 1966, whose executors were brought to justice in the Moors Murders Trial.

From route A635 continue across White Moss and Black Moss, keeping roughly on the watershed between the Saddleworth and Wessenden valleys along a boundary line marked in places by piles of peat. (The boundary is too far west on 1:50,000 maps, but is correct on 1:25,000 maps.) The route runs along the bank of the westernmost reservoir to a packhorse road north of Round Hill, and this is followed to route A62 in Standedge Cutting, 8 miles/12·8 km from Black Hill, 23 miles/36·8 km from Edale.

Standedge Cutting
A mobile tea hut usually occupies a lay-by at the W end of the

cutting, and other refreshments may be obtained at the Great
Western public house at the E end of the cutting, or at the
Coach & Horses ever further E. The Blue Peter Transport Cafe
no longer exists, and the Standedge Service Station is closed and
replaced by the Eagles Nest public house. Overnight
accommodation is harder to find, but it may be possible at the
Coach & Horses. A permanent youth hostel has now been
established at Marsden.

Below Standedge to the west is Cattleshaw Roman Fort, built
by Agricola about AD 80. There are two camps, one inside the
other. The inner one, about $\frac{5}{8}$ of an acre/3 618 sq. metres, is a
rectangle, one of the sides abutting the larger camp, which covers
about 3 acres/1·2 ha. The ramparts are chiefly piled sods, with a
ditch round the outside. The rampart is still 18 ft/5·5 m thick in
places, and is doubled from the north to the south-west corner.
At each corner once stood a raised platform or tower. The fort
seems to have been abandoned about AD 125, in the reign of
Hadrian, when its garrison may have been sent north to work on
the great Roman Wall.

Standedge to Blackstone Edge

Standedge to Windy Hill 4 miles/6·4 km

Standedge presents a formidable obstacle to transport: roads go
over these hills and railways and canals go underneath them. A
double tunnel under Standedge carries the Huddersfield Narrow
Canal between Marsden and Diggle under one arch, and the
railway through the other. This is the highest canal tunnel in
Britain—638 ft/194 m altitude—and also the longest—5,415 yds/
4951 m. There are connections between the canal tunnel and the
railway tunnel by sloping galleries. There is no towpath: boats
were worked through it by 'legging'. The canal is now closed to
traffic.

At Standedge we leave the Peak District National Park. From
the A635 to the A62 at Standedge and through to A640 the
Pennine Way largely follows the boundary between Greater
Manchester and West Yorkshire. A rough track leads us away
from Standedge Cutting and soon gives way to a footpath
following the escarpment of millstone grit and crosses by the
heads of two streams draining SW, past height 1,455 ft/443 m on
Cattleshaw Moor to the Huddersfield road A640. Cross this road
and follow alongside a long wall northerly then westerly round
the north side of White Hill, 1,533 ft/466 m, then north to the
Halifax road A672 near Windy Hill television reflector station.

Windy Hill to Blackstone Edge 2 miles/3·2 km

The boundary now follows the watershed from which streams
descend on one side into Lancashire, and the other into
Yorkshire. Mile after mile of black peat and tussocky grass
stretch around, vast and uninhabited. On both sides lie two of
the most densely populated parts of the world, but these moors
are as lonely as any.

These austere moorlands are of the greatest economic
importance as extensive gathering grounds for the water supply
of the neighbouring thickly populated centres on the adjacent
foothills and lowlands. The soft water running from these peat-

Blackstone Edge to Wadsworth Moor

covered moors first attracted the bleachworks and the weaving sheds, round which the houses still cluster. The smoke from the textile towns adds a tinge to the mountain grass and heather on the hills and the rocks are blackened by soot and grime.

From Windy Hill follow over rough ground along the top of Blackstone Edge as far as the Roman road.

The silence of the moors hereabouts was shattered, for a period of 5 years between autumn 1966 and winter 1971, by the operations of giant earth moving equipment working on the construction of the Trans-Pennine Motorway, M62. The dull roar of traffic can be heard in the deep cutting, and the road's presence is made known at night by the orange glow in the sky from the hundreds of sodium lamps that line its route.

The Pennine Way has been provided for by the construction of a graceful single-span footbridge over the motorway cutting, a three-pin arch with side cantilevers, supporting pre-stressed concrete approach spans, leaping 220 ft/67 m across the abyss. Rumour has it that the bridge was a personal whim of Ernest Marples, the then Minister of Transport and a keen rambler. After all, the interchange of M62 and A672 is not too far away, and little ingenuity would be required to divert the footpath into an underpass below one of the bridges. Fortunately the Pennine Way walker has not been relegated to a subterranean culvert, but elevated to an aerial terraceway over one of the most spectacular motorway projects in the country.

Blackstone Edge
Blackstone Edge, 'The Andes of England' as Defoe called it, towers above the smoke and dirt of industrialism. Here both Lancashire and Yorkshire fall away on either hand; Lancashire more steeply and ruggedly than Yorkshire, with long-distance views along the crest of the Pennines. Legend connects several of the summit rocks with Robin Hood, who, if ever he were here, would see one of the grandest prospects in Lancashire; towns, villages, factories, print works, dye mills and chimneys belching forth smoke, and patches of reservoirs to supply the mills and canals.

The 'Roman Road' over Blackstone Edge

The Pennine Way footbridge. M62 and Windy Hill

'Then I came to Blackstone Edge,' wrote Celia Fiennes of her journey in 1698, 'noted over all England for a dismal high precipice and steep in the ascent and descent on Either End; it's a very moorish ground, all about, and Even just at the top, tho' so high, that you travel on a Causey wch is very troublesome as its a moist ground soe as is unusual on these high hills; they stagnate the aire and hold mist and raines almost perpetualy.'

The Causey is marked on the maps, and always referred to as the Roman road, though archaeologists differ. The gauge of the wheel-ruts is the same as those of the roads of Pompeii and of Hadrian's Wall. With the kerbs, the road is almost 18 ft/5·5 m wide, with perfect paving and a plain camber. There is a deep groove, either cut or worn, in a line of huge stones that run down the centre of the causeway. It may have acted as a guide to a skid which was used to brake vehicles as they descended the steep incline. The road is now more or less overgrown with whortle and crowberry, but the best preserved section is found at the start of the descent into Lancashire. At the summit the road is unmistakable, and appears to have been cut through solid rock, with paving superimposed.

After you have left the gritstone outcrop of Blackstone Edge proper and continued along the boundary ridge, there will cross your path at right angles a well paved and ancient road near a cross called the Aiggin Stone.

This track now at your feet is the presumed Roman road; Roman coins have been found nearby, and certainly the Romans did have a road from Manchester to Aldburgh which must have crossed the Edge near this point.

Blackstone Edge Roman Road

Mr. H. C. Collins has made a special study of the roads in this district and says: 'It is not "Roman" in pavement, although the width of the road and of the tyre marks have been compared with other Roman examples.' He continues:

'If these centre grooved troughstones have no relation to Roman roads, they certainly have very humble origins, and can be compared with any packhorse 'causey' track on the

Pennines, where they are the main feature. But some say that this cannot be a packhorse track because of the pavement on either side of the centre groove stones, the lateral fosses, the cut-and-cover drains, and kerbstones. The latter are referred to in Adam Watkin's 'Observations' (1791), where he writes: "For many ages and to the middle of this century, a causeway, about two feet broad, paved with rounded pebbles, was all that a man or horse could travel upon, particularly in the winter season through both Lancashire and Cheshire."

'There is an example of this type of causeway only a few yards from the Roman road, which it joins at the Aiggin Stone. It has a line of centre groove stones, some of them far larger and cruder than any on the "Roman" road. It has a pebble pavement on either side and kerbstones. The "Roman" road would appear to be a development from this early structure, a widening of the pavement section so that it could take the increasing amount of traffic, including carts; a traffic growing in volume with the momentum of the Industrial Revolution. These two types of causeways—the horseways and the cartways—were in continual use.'

The Aiggin Stone is a guiding-post on the summit of the 'Roman' road at the junction of the older packhorse road. On the stone is carved a Latin cross and the intials 'I.T.' An engineers map of 1880 gives it the name of the Aiggin Stone (gg pronounced as j). Aiggin could be a corruption of Agger, a Latin word meaning an earthwork, fortress or mound (Aggerere = to heap up) or it could also be no more than the 'Edge' or 'Edging' Stone (which rhymes with Aiggin) or summit of the pass.

From the Aiggin Stone our route follows the narrower causeway leading northwest. This horseway was superseded by the wider 'Roman' cartway, but was still used by the loaded limegals because the 'Roman' road was so steep—in one part about 1 in 4½. (Limegal was a packhorse carrying exported lime from impoverished Clitheroe; Gal is a corruption of Galloway, the Scottish district where the more sturdy of these small horses were bred.)

Among the uncut natural rock outcrops above the road can be

seen the chisel marks on blocks which the road-builders and menders almost shaped as causey stones but abandoned them because of fracture. One wayside boulder hereabouts has crude crosses carved into it, a forerunner of the more ambitiously carved and erected post such as the Aiggin Stone.

This causeway leads to Broadhead Drain, and this is crossed and followed northwards to a fence and a gate, then left to some quarries and the White House Inn on the A58 Rochdale-Halifax road above Littleborough (7 miles/11·2 km from Standedge, 30 miles/48 km from Edale). Liquid refreshment and luncheons are available during licensed hours.

The White House Inn stands at the summit of the modern road. The old coach road from Littleborough joins here, but it is now overgrown with grass. An Act of Parliament passed on 14th January, 1734, brought to an end the use of this road, stating, 'by reason of the nature of the soil and the narrowness of the road in several places, and of the many heavy carriages frequently passing, it has become so exceedingly deep and ruinous that in winter season, and often in summer, many parts thereof are impassable for wagons, carts, and other wheeled carriages and very dangerous to travellers'. The same Act marked the cut of the new road 'for repairing, and widening the road from the town of Rochdale, in the County Palatine of Lancaster, over a certain craggy mountain called Blackstone Edge'.

White House to Stoodley Pike 5 miles/8 km
Climb the road beyond the White House Inn and pass through the gates on the left at the summit, along the western embankment of Blackstone Edge Reservoir and the watershed by the Regulation Drain, then by Light Hazzles and the farthest point of Warland Reservoir. Some of these man-made lakes are reservoirs of drinking water, some provide for canals, and some for great industrial undertakings, and all are resting places for mallard and gulls.

Down to the right leads Turvin Clough, once the haunt of the Yorkshire Coiners, led by David Hartley. Spanish coins and Portuguese moidores were common currency in those days, and the coiners clipped the edges of these gold coins and put them back into circulation. With the chippings they made English sovereigns, and they were received by sheep-keepers, bankers, mill-masters and others at advantageous rates. In time, however, the government put a customs officer on the track of the coiners, but he learned too much for his safety and was killed one night by one of the gang. However, one of these gave news of Hartley's whereabouts and he was captured and later hanged at York.

On reaching the Warland Drain past the farthest reservoir turn east to a parish boundary, and continue along that line north-easterly to a wall which is followed to Stoodley Pike, an obelisk commemorating the Battle of Waterloo (5 miles/8 km from White House Inn; 35 miles/56 km from Edale).

Stoodley Pike is visible from afar, and stands 120 ft/56 m high on the top of a 1,300 ft/381 m ridge. The Pike has a faintly prophetic reputation with local people, there having been a series of collapses, replacements and repairs which were coincidental with world events.

The monument was erected to commemorate the Peace of Ghent and the abdication of Napoleon in 1814. It was finished after the Battle of Waterloo, when peace was finally established in 1815. In 1854, the day the Russian ambassador left London before the declaration of war with Russia, the Pike collapsed, and was rebuilt again when peace was declared in 1856. The cause of the collapse was thought to be erosion of the earth at the base. A lightning conductor was fixed during the first years of the Boer War, and the Pike collapsed again on the morning of 11th November, 1918, just before peace was declared in World War 1.

Mankinholes

Before reaching the Pike a footpath leads down to Mankinholes from near height 1,208 ft/368 m, leaving the summit ridge at a gate in the wall we have followed from Warland Drain. Through this gateway is a carved wayside stone, with 'Te Deum Laudamus' beautifully chiselled in an old style, presumably the mark of a religious man who combined church with estate business.

The path leading down westwards to Mankinholes and the youth hostel is known as the 'Long Stoup' or the 'Long Drag' and is the easiest way off the top of the moor. It circles to ease the gradient, and is marked at intervals by tall stone pillars which act as guide posts to the track of causey stones.

The Long Drag is now partly overgrown, but in its stones lie one of the saddest stories of Lancashire—the Cotton Famine. This road was built by men whose stomachs were empty and their families starving. It is an example of how relief work was planned by a few of the best mill owners before the days of unemployment benefits.

In this case Honest John Fielden, the Unitarian philanthropist admired by Shaftesbury, provided the work of building a road to Stoodley Pike so that he could drive his private carriage to the top of the ridge from his home at Dobroyd Castle near Todmorden. It was not necessary work, but it was some return for money which he gave in terms of relief which could be called wages until the cotton mills could be reopened.

At the bottom of the steep scarp slope the track bears right towards Mankinholes village, where there is a long stone watering trough which would once serve a whole 'gang' of packhorses at a time. Mankinholes was one of the first meeting places of the Quakers, despite suppression in the reign of Charles. The earliest record of their meetings was in the house of one Joshua Laycock on 3rd December, 1667. They rented a croft nearby as a burial ground for 'a twopence of Silver' yearly rent for a term of 900 years. This can be traced although it is built upon. There is a gravestone in the wall of one of the buildings with the inscription 'J.S. 1685'.

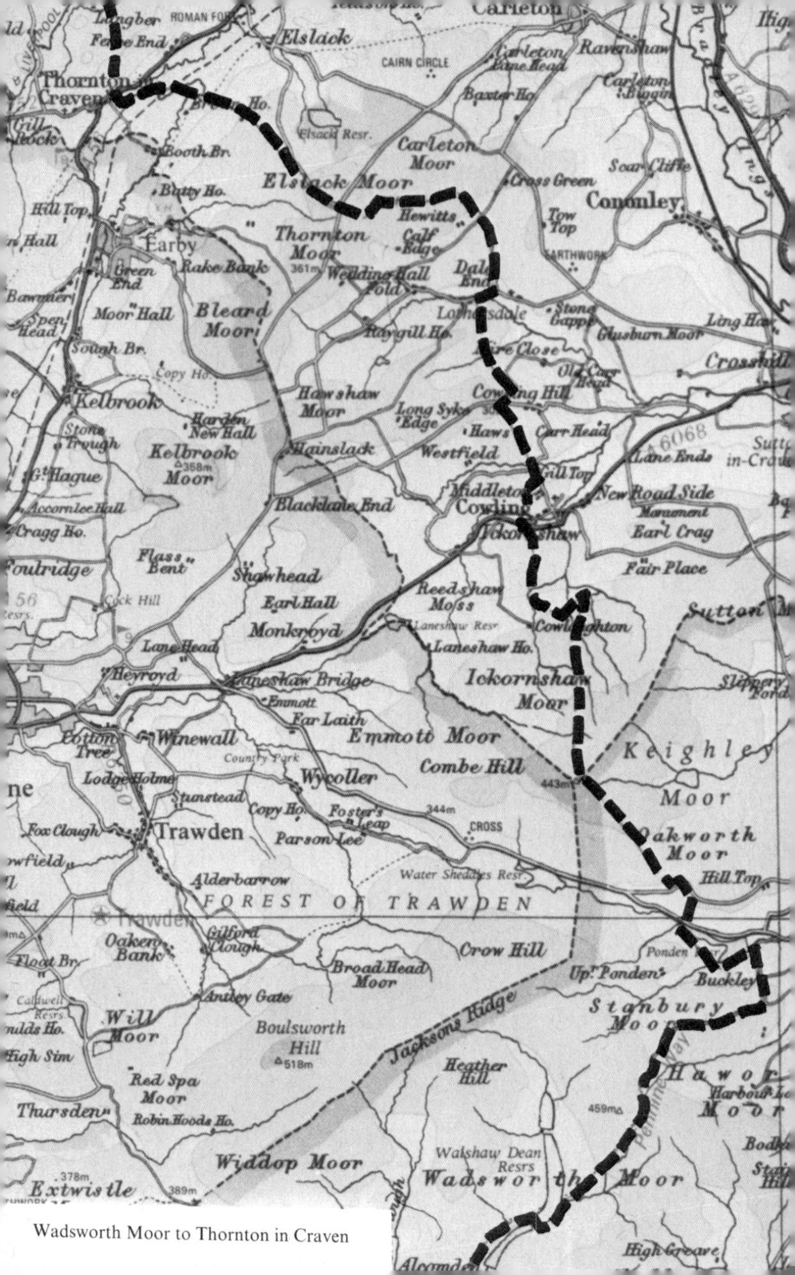

Wadsworth Moor to Thornton in Craven

Stoodley Pike to Colden 5 miles/8 km

From Mankinholes to the next youth hostel at Earby is a distance of about 20 miles/32 km, and a 1:25,000 scale map is preferable for this next stage of the journey.

Climb the flagged causey of the Long Drag from the village to the summit ridge, then bear north to Stoodley Pike. If this monument has already been visited, much time can be saved by taking the track below the scarp slope to Edge End Moor, by the westerly flank of that hill.

From Stoodley Pike a path runs east, passing a good spring after about 200 yds/182 m, and then reaches a stile in a wall. Turn left at the stile and follow the wall down to a track, then follow this northerly round the east and north sides of Edge End Moor, eventually descending to the A646 Burnley-Halifax road, the canal, river, and railway.

This very narrow gorge of the River Calder has cotton manufactures, clothing mills, dye works and factories crowded into the valley, and the smoke and smell of industrial effluent fill the lungs. Stern terrace houses and gritstone walls climb the side of the valley, which is an important link between the cotton towns of Lancashire and the woollen towns of Yorkshire.

Turn eastwards along the road for a few yards, and then left under a railway bridge by a path that zig-zags up the steep hillside. Looking back now we can see the outline of Stoodley Pike, two miles/3·2 km distant.

The slope levels out, and at about 1,050 ft/315 m the Long Causeway is crossed. This metalled road was formed during the Middle Ages as the main traffic route between Lancashire and Yorkshire, and it is joined throughout its length by numerous other tracks serving all the towns in these Pennines.

The crowded life of the narrow valleys is now left behind, and vast stretches of moorland lie beyond. The path soon drops steeply into the valley of Colden Water near New Delight, crosses the stream by an old packhorse bridge, then climbs again to Colden and a spur of Heptonstall Moor.

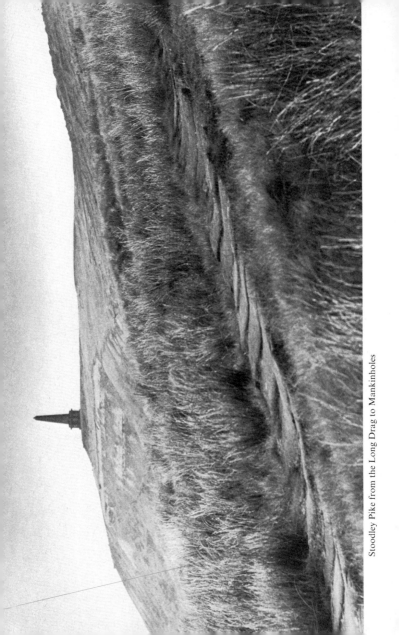

Stoodley Pike from the Long Drag to Mankinholes

Colden to Withens Height 6 miles/9·6 km

The Pennine Way from Colden bears north-westerly round height 1,284 ft/398 m on Heptonstall Moor, then northerly across the outflows from Lower Gorple and Widdop Reservoirs to the Hebden road. A turn to the right on this road will bring you to the Pack Horse Inn, and when you have refreshed yourself, retrace your steps for a distance of about half a mile/0·8 km and then turn east through an iron gate on the track to the Walshaw Dean Reservoirs, water supply for Halifax.

Cross the dam at the head of the first reservoir, then turn left beside the stone built drain. At the crossing of Black Clough follow the track north-easterly to Withens Height and Withens Farm, where there is a fresh-water spring. We have now come 10 miles/16 km from Stoodley Pike, a distance of 45 miles/72 km from Edale.

Withens Height to Ponden 3 miles/5 km

High Withens is the site Emily Brontë chose for "Wuthering Heights", a wild spot overlooking endless miles of rolling moorland, sinister and sombre in mist and rain. These gaunt hills are immortalised by the writings of the famous Brontë sisters. The scenery of the hills is not grand nor romantic, yet it is from these hills that the sisters drew their inspiration. Charlotte once wrote: 'My sister Emily loved the moors . . . she found in the bleak solitude many and dear delights; and not the least and best loved was liberty. Liberty was the breath of Emily's nostrils; without it she perished.'

Leave Withens behind and take the track leading down to Master Stones, which then becomes a lane, but after 0·25 mile/ 0·4 km turn left (north) along a footpath to Buckley and Ponden Reservoir. Take the track along the south side of the reservoir, which becomes a footpath beyond Ponden Hall to Whitestone, then a lane again to the road. Ponden Hall was the 'Thrushcross Grange" of "Wuthering Heights." Now it provides refreshments and accommodation, and tuition in handloom weaving.

A museum dedicated to the Brontë sisters is to be found at Haworth, 3 miles/5 km to the E of Ponden, where there is also a youth hostel.

Ponden to Cowling 4 miles/6·4 km
From the Colne-Haworth road cross up Dean Fields to the
higher road, then bear westerly round Crag Bottom, taking the
first track on the right up on to Oakworth Moor. Follow a
broken wall north-westerly over Old Bess and Bare Hill on
Keighley Moor, to near height 1,455 ft/443 m and a parish
boundary. From this point descend northerly over Ickornshaw
Moor to reach a footpath, which bears westerly to Lumb and
then north to the Keighley-Colne road A6068 in Cowling village
(7 miles/11·2 km from Withens; total 52 miles/83·6 km from
Edale).

The Black Bull Hotel almost opposite provides refreshments.
Cowling is a good place to obtain supplies, for Earby youth
hostel 7 miles/11·2 km further has no store and members must
cook their own meals. Alternative accommodation in this area is
hard to find.

Cowling to Thornton 7 miles/11·2 km
Take the path beside the Black Bull Hotel car park, descend to
the village street, pass behind some buildings to the school and
follow the minor road to the hamlet of Middleton, the birthplace
of Philip Snowden. A bronze plaque above the place where he
was born says, 'In this cottage was born, on July 16th, 1864, the
Right Honourable Philip Snowden PC, First Viscount of
Ickornshaw, three times Chancellor of the Exchequer of Great
Britain.' Philip Snowden was one of the brains of Ramsey
MacDonald's Labour Party Government.

Beyond Gill Bridge near Middleton is a confusing series of
lanes and footpaths. Turn left along the lane beside the northern
bank of the stream at Gill Bridge to the ruins of an old mill, then
turn right through a stile and by path uphill passing Stubbing
and High Windmill farms to reach Cowling Hill Lane. Follow
the road opposite steeply downhill, and at the second sharp
corner enter the fields and cross the Surgill Beck, pass Woodhead
Farm and then descend steeply to Lothersdale, a village where
grey houses cluster about the mills by the stream. This deep
valley in the heart of the moors gave the Quakers safe refuge in

the time of Charles II, and Friends from afar still visit the quaint little Meeting House. The church stands high on the hillside, and beyond is Stone Gappe, the 'Gateshead Hall' of 'Jane Eyre'. This is a fine mansion where Charlotte Brontë spent a miserable three months as governess in 1839.

In Lothersdale quite close to the Hare and Hounds will be found a Countryside Commission map and a Pennine Way signpost, which points through a farmyard to a lane. At the end of the lane the route follows field paths to Kirk Sykes and Hewitts Farms. The way now to be followed to Pinhaw Beacon is a little difficult at the beginning, and a word at either of the nearby farms may save much time and energy.

Pass through a gate at Kirk Sykes and follow a boundary wall for a short way to a stile, then strike west to Pinhaw Beacon, 1,273 ft/338 m. From the trig station on the summit descend southwest through a swathe in the heather on a line marked by cairns to an old quarry road which leads north-west to three lane ends on Elslack Moor.

Follow the Elslack road for ½-mile/0·8 km, then bear north-westerly by Thornton Wood and Brown House to Thornton in Craven, a distance of 7 miles/11·2 km from Cowling and 59 miles/ 95 km from Edale).

Earby youth hostel can be reached by the footpath from the Elslack road, and this develops into a lane leading south-west to the busy little cotton town of Earby. The hostel by Wentcliff Brook was once the home of the late Katherine Bruce Glasier, a woman who was devoted to the interests of young people and the cause of international peace. It was given by her trustees to the Association, and opened in 1958. The hostel is small and comfortable, and has attractive gardens. There are no meals provided, but there are ample facilities for self-cookers. There is not store, but there are shops in the town one mile/1·6 km from the hostel. Alternatively, the Manor Hotel in Thorton in Craven will provide bed and breakfast at a reasonable price.

Thornton in Craven to Malham

Thornton in Craven

The mass of Millstone Grit that has shaped the scenery for the
last 60 miles/96·5 km now gives way to outcrops of shale and
limestone. The rough moorlands and peat hags are now left
behind, and pleasant footpaths lead us forward beside canal and
river through dairy farming country to Malham, 11 miles/
17·6 km distant.

   Thornton is in a charming setting, and the 4 miles/6·4 km to
Gargrave are really delightful. From the village green on the A56
road take the shaded Cam Lane northwards, which degenerates
into a track to Langber Farm, but bear right on a footpath
leading to the Leeds and Liverpool Canal. The towpath is
followed for a short distance, and this stretch along the canal
bank is at its best during the week, as at fishing season weekends
it is very popular with anglers. Keep to the towpath, passing on
the left the village of East Marton, where an old double-decker
bridge carries the A59 over the canal. This bridge is 89 miles/
143 km from Liverpool and $38\frac{1}{2}$ miles/62 km from Leeds.

   Leave the canal bank $\frac{1}{4}$-mile/0·4 km beyond Williamston
Bridge by a footpath. which shortly regains the lane again.
Follow it easterly for another $\frac{1}{4}$-mile/0·4 km, then take the field
paths past Great Meadow Plantation in an almost straight line
north-easterly to Scaleber and the railway cutting near Gargrave.
Cross the bridge and take the footpath bearing right, emerging
near the church of St Andrew by the River Aire ($4\frac{1}{2}$ miles/7·2 km
from Thornton; $63\frac{1}{2}$ miles/102 km from Edale).

Gargrave

Tradition asserts that Gargrave once had seven churches, all of
which were destroyed by raiding Scots except that remaining,
which they spared because it was dedicated to their national
saint. Other travellers who have come this way were Romans,
Angles, Danes and Norsemen, for the Aire Gap was, and still is,
a busy crossing through these Pennine Hills.

East Marton Bridge over the Leeds and Liverpool Canal

The road and river and the long green run side by side in this busy village. The village shops offer the last opportunities for obtaining supplies for the next 30 miles/48 km, and meals and refreshments are widely available.

Airedale

From Gargrave go up West Street to cross the canal on the N side of the village, and by track and footpath over Eshton Moor. Here we enter the Yorkshire Dales National Park. Leave the lane at the end of the wood and climb the hill, keeping a wall on your right and trig point on your left. At the end of the wall pass through a gate and descend to join the River Aire by the Airton-Eshton road. Cross the river by a footbridge and follow the west bank upstream for ½-mile/0·8 km to Newfield Bridge, where cross the river again. Climb the stile by the bridge and follow the east bank of the River Aire to Airton and Hanlith.

Airton is a cosy little place nestling round its village green, upon which is a squatters' house, one of the best examples still standing in the country. In the seventeenth century when housing was difficult, a homeless person could apply to the Quarter Sessions, who with the consent of the township concerned, could grant him permission to build a house with a small garden on the commons.

The Canons of Bolton Priory once had a mill here, and the old mill by the bridge has now been converted into holiday flats.

A further 1½ miles/2·4 km from Airton by the sparkling Aire brings us to Hanlith, and across the river not far away is Kirkby Malham with its interesting church. The church is most famous for the dubious signatures of Oliver Cromwell, who witnessed a marriage here on 17th January, 1655. There is also a war memorial to the son of Cromwell's friend, Honest John Lambert. John Lambert, who was born at Calton Hall near Airton, helped to win the crowning victory of the Civil War at Worcester in 1651.

Take the lane on the west bank of the river from Hanlith bridge, which leads past an old water mill and Aire Head Springs to Malham village, 6½ miles/10 km from Gargrave.

Malham

Malham is an oasis in a wilderness of limestone, having many picturesque whitewashed buildings nestling round a wide green. The infant River Aire runs through the middle of the village and is crossed by no less than five quaint bridges. In monastic times Malham east of the beck belonged to Bolton Priory, while west of the stream was part of the Fountains Abbey estate.

Malham is an ideal place at which to spend a rest day, before we continue on the next stage of our Pennine Way journey. Some 70 miles/112 km have now been covered, and the next suitable accommodation is at Stainforth, 12 miles/19 km further on.

A profitable day can be spent around Malham for there are many places of interest to visit. Bed and breakfast accommodation may be obtained at the Listers Arms or the Buck Hotel or neighbouring farms, or there is the superb youth hostel. The Memorial Youth Hostel, opened in 1938, was designed by John Dower, a man who did so much for the foundation of National Parks. The Buck Hotel once had a surprising collection of big game heads, horns and antlers, but these have long been removed, along with a mosaic floor which was given by John Ruskin.

Gordale Scar

Impressive Gordale Scar, $1\frac{1}{4}$ miles/2 km E of the village, should be visited whilst at Malham. The road twists and turns to Gordale Bridge, where just south of the road is the pretty fall of Janet's Foss. Turn off at the farm in the dip and follow the little beck across the fields until it swings suddenly between the towering cliffs of the defile. The approach to the Scar is impressive. The walls of the ravine shut out the sun and cast an eerie light on the scene. A stream gushes out of a square window high up in the limestone face, and cascades over fantastic rocks and rough-hewn steps, shut in by the precipitous cliffs 300 ft/ 91 m high. The noise of the waterfalls reverberates through this fantastic gorge. Wordsworth declared it to be one of the grandest objects in nature, while Gray admitted that, 'I stayed there not without shuddering, a quarter of an hour; and thought my

The approach to Gordale Scar

The overhanging cliffs of Gordale Scar

Gordale Scar from the top of the falls

trouble richly repaid for the impression which will last with life.'

Professor Trueman, in his admirable 'Geology and Scenery,' says of Gordale: 'It is probably a cavern of which the roof has collapsed. The walls are steep and mostly bare, the clean joint planes making great precipices where they cut through the massive beds; in several places the walls overhang slightly and at one point a remnant of a roof still remains. Near this is a small waterfall, for some water still flows along the surface, though the supply is much reduced owing to the fact that the greater part of the stream sinks below ground some way up the valley, to reach the surface again near the mouth of the gorge. Here then is an old cave which has lost its roof and has almost lost its water floor; the stream first passed underground to form the cave which is still represented by the gorge, and later found a still lower path. So the water is continuously being short-circuited.'

The waterfall at the head of the gorge can be climbed on the left-hand side unless the stream is in flood, and the beck followed up to Mastiles Lane, joining the road from Malham near Street Gate.

Geology and Botany of Craven

Gordale Scar and Malham Cove were caused by the vertical displacement of the Middle Craven Fault. The old beds of carboniferous limestone were thus thrust above the sea-level to form a 300 ft/91 m high wall, 40 miles/64 km long, above the younger gritstones. The cliffs were exposed to rain and river erosion; the limestone being soluble in even such a weak acid as rain water which has absorbed carbon dioxide from the atmosphere. Water sinks into the fissures of the rock and proceeds to form underground caverns and water-courses, which in turn affect the surface drainage, drawing streams down through 'swallow holes' and opening further caves. Drops of water percolating through the roofs of caverns form 'icicles' of calcium carbonate—stalactites; or falling to the floor evaporate to form stalagmites.

The underlying rock of these Craven uplands affect the soil, grass and woodland, the farming pattern and the local building materials. Heather, bilberry and bracken like the acid peat of gritstone and will not grow on limestone, but a wonderful range of flowers will grow on limestone that will not grow on the gritstone moorlands.

Commonplace flowers of spring in Craven are mountain pansies—both yellow and purple; birds e'een or mealy primrose; yellow rockrose and heartsease, cowslips and purple orchises, violets, primroses; aromatic snowy Sweet Cicily; Canterbury Bells in pale lilac spikes; blue Meadow Cranesbill and crimson Bloody Cranesbill; tiny Dove Foot, Brookline and Forgetmenots; Spotted Monkey Musk; Bistort, the pink passion dock; and Easter Magiant—much used by dales-women for making of herb pudding.

Rarer flowers bloom in deep clefts of the limestone rocks— Geranium Robert, Yellow Toadflax, Red Valerian and Hartstongue ferns.

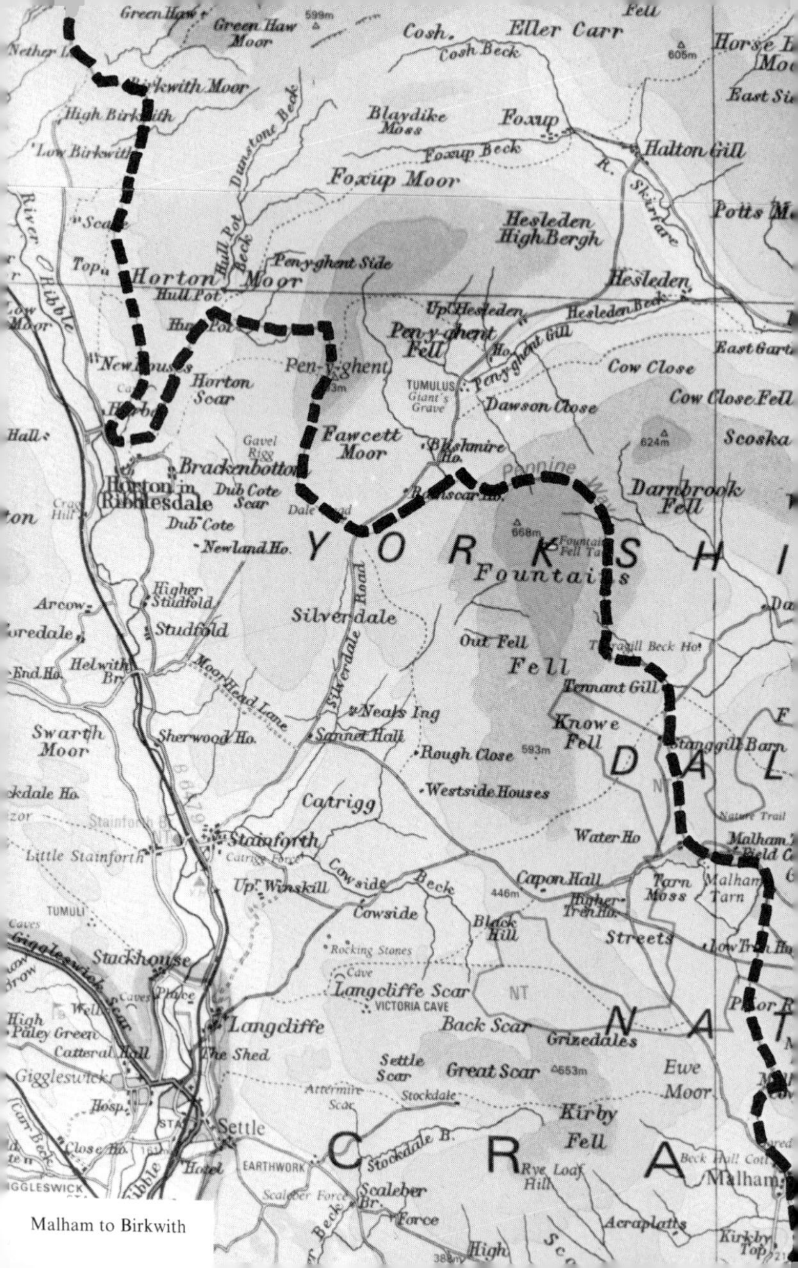

Malham to Birkwith

Malham Cove

Leaving Malham take the westernmost road that climbs up to
Ewe Moor. About halfway up the steep climb a path diverges
from the road through a gateway, leading to the Malham Cove.
Approaching the Cove through the pastures you can see regular
mounds of rock forming Iron Age field boundaries, whilst
cultivation terraces can be seen on the far hillside. They are not
very easy to see, for the eye is drawn continually towards the
Cove.

A vast amphitheatre of cliffs is our destination; a wall of rock
which towers vertically to a height of 300 ft/91 m. A crystal clear
stream emerges from a long low arch at the base of the cliff and
threads its way through clumps of oak and alder.

At one time a river flowed from Malham Tarn on the moor
above and poured over the edge of the Cove in a single
tremendous waterfall, doubtless magnificent in time of flood.
However, no water now falls over the cliff. The stream which
drains Malham Tarn disappears underground at Water Sinks,
destined to emerge at Aire Head Springs below Malham village
and not at the foot of the Cove as many believe. Experiments
have proved that the stream from the Cove is one which
disappears near a disused smelt-mill south-west of Malham Tarn.

From the foot of the Cove scramble up the steep slopes on the
left-hand side and gain the top by a stile in the wall. Here, above
the Cove, is a vast limestone pavement, deeply fissured and
dazzling white in the sunshine, strange as mountains of the
moon. This regular pattern of joints and crevices is called by the
Norse name 'grykes' and they leave between them 'clints' which
have in their depths a wonderful growth of ferns—harts' tongue
fern, wood sorrel and other plants, and stunted hawthorn bushes.

The dry river valley still remains above the Cove and this can
be followed up to Malham Tarn, but the Pennine Way footpath
lies just east of the dry valley. From the gate in the wall follow
another wall which runs at right-angles up the valley side. At a

Approach to Malham Cove

stile in the wall turn north and cross Prior Rakes to Ha Mire Plantation.

Of the dry valley Dr Raistrick in 'The Face of North-West Yorkshire' says: 'The melt water from the snowfall and glaciers during and for a long time after the Ice Age was compelled to flow on the surface, as all the joints in the limestone were sealed by ice to a great depth. It was then that the dry valley was formed as the Cove was cut back as a huge waterfall. For centuries after the final disappearance of the ice the cover of boulder clay allowed some of the upland drainage to flow that way, but now the clay cover has been pierced and all the drainage goes underground.'

Malham Tarn

At Water Sinks the outlet from Malham Tarn percolates through limestone rubble adjacent to a wall, when it ought to run down the dry valley. Along here are numerous sink holes, marking the line where the impervious Silurian shales come into contact with the limestone of the Craven Fault. These shales support Malham Tarn, the highest lake in the Pennines, 1,229 ft/374 m above sea level. A blue-grey mirror on the fell tops, the 150 acre/60 ha lake is the property of the National Trust, with an abundance of fish and fresh water life.

The Pennine Way track skirts the eastern side of the Tarn and passes through the grounds of Malham Tarn House, a late Georgian style mansion occupying a commanding position overlooking the Tarn. The house was built by Walter Morrison in 1850, and here he lived for 64 years. A millionaire and Liberal MP—he sat in Parliament for 40 years—he entertained many distinguished visitors: John Ruskin, John Stuart Mill, Charles Darwin and Charles Kingsley. Kingsley began writing 'Water Babies' while staying here, and many local places are recognisable in the novel.

The house and its 800 acre/323 ha estate was presented to the National Trust by Mrs Hutton Croft in 1946, and was subsequently leased from the Trust in 1948 by the Council for the Promotion of Field Studies, and accommodates about 50

The cliffs of Malham Cove

Iron Age
Field System

Malham

R. Aire

Limestone clints above the Cove

The dry valley above the Cove

Malham Tarn House

Fountains Fell from Malham Moor

Fountains Fell

Tennant Gill

Stanggill Barn

students. This is now a wonderful centre for natural history students, ornithologists, botanists, and geologists. Flowers and mosses grow here which are found nowhere else in England, so please do not trespass.

Malham Tarn to Fountains Fell 3 miles/4·8 km

Pass Malham Tarn House by the drive to Water Houses and turn northwards on a footpath over Malham Moor. After ½-mile 0·8 km the track is blocked by a stone wall, but follow this wall north-easterly, crossing two other walls to reach a gate on a cart track near Stanggill Barn. Turn left through this gate to the Arncliffe road, which follow north for a short distance, then take the track bearing left to Tennant Gill Farm.

An old mine track leads from the farm and ascends Fountains Fell. This track is not very clear, and the beacons are not very good. In bad weather take a compass bearing north-west from Tennant Gill and this will lead you to Dale Head House. At about 1,650 ft/503 m the track crosses the Tennant Gill and bears north, and you can notice the transition from limestone turf to the tussocky grass of an acid gritstone moor. There are many shake-holes and streams at this level, but the going improves as you reach higher ground.

The gritstone lies like a cap on these montains of limestone, and cause them to be hollow inside with caves and potholes. In the rock strata are thin seams of coal, and the track we are following climbs to an outcrop on the summit of Fountains Fell.

Fountains Fell to Penyghent 4 miles/6·4 km

On the north side of the fell the track bends westerly then south-westerly, leading down to the Silverdale Road at Dale Head. Stainforth is some 3½ miles/5·6 km down this road to the south. There is a youth hostel just south of the village, and the Craven Heifer Inn in Stainforth offers accommodation and meals. The youth hostel was built about 1848 and purchased by the Association in 1944. In the garden are to be seen a number of bee-boles—cavities in the thick stone wall to hold bee hives.

If you stay at the hostel here do not fail to see the old one-arch bridge, a fine relic of packhorse days, which spans the River Ribble in one gracious sweep. This 400-year old bridge was formerly on the line of an ancient track, considered the shortest route between York and Lancaster. It has belonged to the National Trust since 1931. While at Stainforth do not fail to see Stainforth Force to the south of the bridge and also Catrigg Force, a fine cataract in a narrow gorge approached up a stoney lane leading east from the village.

Since leaving Fountains Fell, Penyghent, 2,273 ft/694 m, has dominated the view, and from Dale Head Farm we commence its ascent.

From the farm a track leads to Churn Milk Hole, a notable depression on the left of the track where a small stream emerges and sinks. Though only a small cave, its boulders are loose and dangerous.

Leave the track by the pothole and continue forward to a wall, and follow this up the sheer gritstone crags to Penyghent summit cairn—a steep climb. From the breezy top—Penyghent means 'Hill of the Winds'—can be seen bare hills and miles of open country. Fountains Fell dominates the southern scene, while flat-topped Ingleborough lies due west, with Whernside and other lofty moors beyond.

Penyghent is a mass of limestone capped by a slab of millstone grit, and it is this which forms the crags around the hill. The screes of these crags are deep channels in the side of the hill; they began to appear after a cloudburst about 1930, and are now 10 ft/3 m deep and 20 ft/6 m wide, Many furious storms have caused the base of Penyghent to be honeycombed by hidden passages and waterworn channels, while in a bad winter snowdrifts may form on the top to a depth of 30 ft/9 m and remain until June.

The three peaks of Penyghent, 2,273 ft/694 m, Ingleborough, 2,373 ft/723 m, and Whernside, 2,419 ft/736 m, dominate the Pennine scene, and they seem to challenge the human spirit. The walk that encompasses all their summits is a classic of its kind. It was first recorded as being done by two school teachers on a fine night in July, 1887, a distance of 27 miles/43 km in 10 hours.

Hunt Pot, on the flank of Penyghent

Penyghent and Hull Pot

The descent to Horton in Ribblesdale from Hull Pot

Penyghent from the green lane to Horton

There is now an annual race over these fells, always on the last
Sunday in April, the fastest circuit being 2 hrs 29 mins 53 secs
set by Jeff Norman in 1974. Norman succeeded after 8 years to
become the first athlete to break 2½ hours for the course, and his
1974 title was his sixth successive win for the event.

Penyghent to Horton 3 miles/4·8 km

Our route follows the wall along the summit ridge north towards
Plover Hill. It is difficult to find shelter on these raking slopes,
and the drystone walls are no help, for they were built to allow
the wind to blow through their chinks instead of knocking them
down.

The 4 mile/6·4 km descent to Horton starts at the saddle
between Penyghent and Plover Hill by an old miners track
leading down Penyghent Side and, though steep, the descent is
not difficult.

There are many potholes along this side of Penyghent which
vary in depth from 60 ft/18 m to 210 ft/60 m. They are classed as
very difficult, severe, and super-severe, and no exploration of them
should be undertaken without proper equipment and experienced
guides.

Descend the miners track, pass through a fell gate, turn left,
and then through another gate where a path leads past Hunt Pot,
a narrow rift 15 ft × 6 ft × 200 ft (4·5 m × 1·8 m × 60 m) deep.
In a short distance the path passes through another wicket gate
and reaches a stone hut. A short distance upstream, circled by a
wire fence, is the tremendous cavity of Hull Pot, 'like the inside
of a great Gothic castle, the high ruinous walls of which were left
standing after the roof had fallen in'. It is 300 ft long, 60 ft wide.
and 60 ft deep (90 m × 18 m × 18m).

The beck that feeds this pothole mostly disappears
underground before it reaches the rim of the cavity, and the
subdued rumblings of the hidden beck can be heard. In times of
heavy rainfall the stream overflows the crack in its limestone
bed and then falls into the Pot over the rim, the volume being too
great to flow underground. If the rainstorm continues for an
exceptional length of time the Pot fills right to the brim, and may

even 'boil over', then it will suddenly empty like a bathtub.

In ordinary times the Hull Pot stream emerges from a huge cave at the foot of Douk Ghyll Scar a mile/1·6 km distant, and when the Pot 'boils over' the overflow runs down the hollows to fall over the Scar in a thin and slender cascade.

From the gate near Hull Pot a rough walled-in green lane descends gradually to Horton in Ribblesdale, 2 miles/3·2 km away (14 miles/22·5 km from Malham: total 84 miles/135 km).

Horton in Ribblesdale

Horton is a little place of whitewashed and sombre grey cottages haphazardly sited round a stream which feeds the Ribble. The charming little church is a focal point, to which we are led by two quaint lych gates, each with a roof made of two great stone slabs.

The church of St Oswald still retains many primitive Norman features, though it was restored in 1400 when the sturdy perpendicular west tower was added. The Norman nave chancel and aisles are all under one roof, whose leaded covering was obtained from the mining of crude ore from Hull Pot. In the west window of the tower is a fragment of stained glass showing the mitred head of Thomas à Becket, whose murder was news when the church was young. On the glass are the words 'Thomas Cantaur'.

Horton has a good inn, The Crown, while the Penyghent Cafe between the inn and the church provides good meals and refreshments. The Cafe owners will also be able to direct the walker to local bed and breakfast accommodation and a camp site in the village.

Horton to Hawes 14 miles/22·5 km

The Pennine Way route from Horton into Wensleydale starts out on the green lane from the Crown Inn (marked New Inn on the map) leading north, passing Sell Gill Holes after one mile/1·6 km. A natural bridge divides the two entrances to this pothole, which is 210 ft/64 m deep. A little farther north lies Jackdaw Hole, where trees fringe a 70 ft × 40 ft/21 m × 12 m opening.

The green lane is followed on to Birkwith Moor, where the

Penyghent, from Horton in Ribblesdale

Penyghent and the Crown Inn, Horton in Ribblesdale

The green lane from Horton to Birkwith Moor

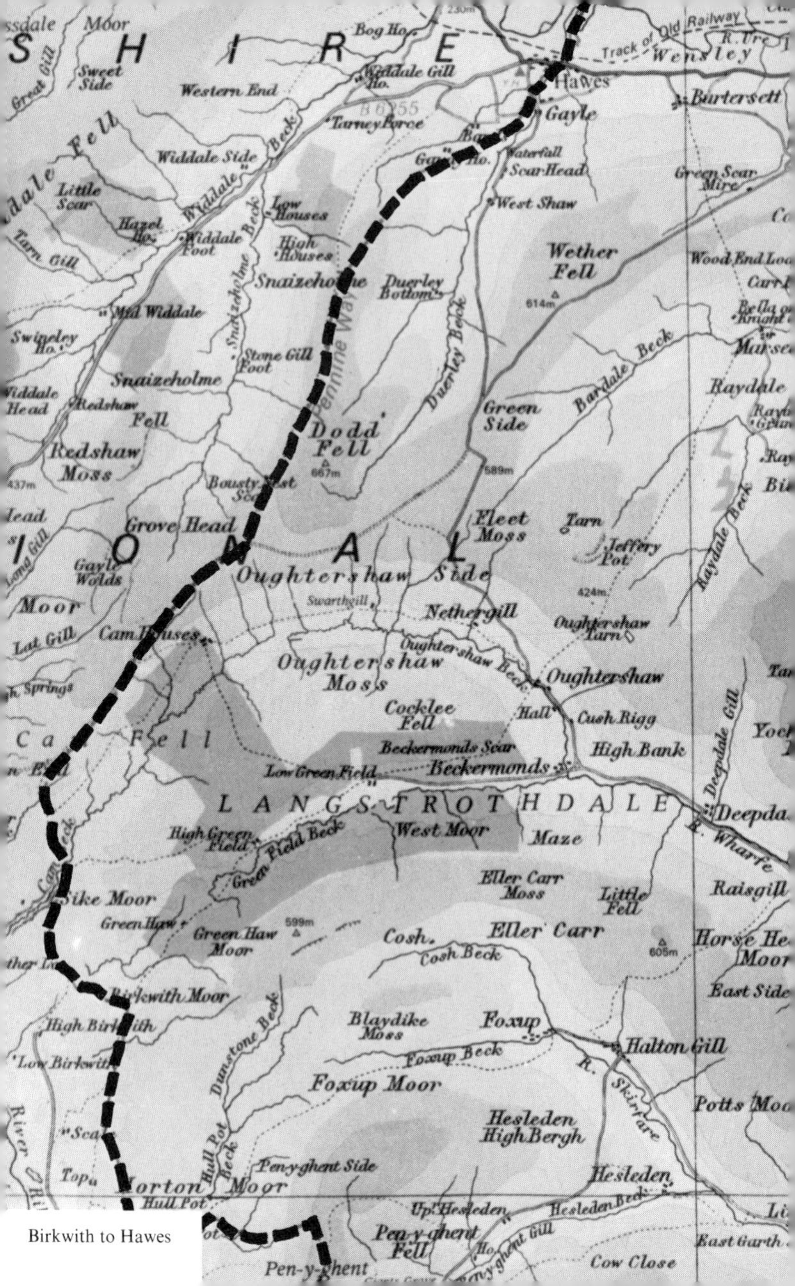

Birkwith to Hawes

official route is rather complex to follow until Old Ing Farm is reached. Leave the green lane at a gate in a wall, go westerly over a low hill to a barn, then follow a wall to a track which leads to Old Ing.

Old Ing will be the start of the possible line of a proposed long-distance footpath link from the Pennine Way to the Lake District. This will give walkers the opportunity of proceeding to the Lakes by way of a scenic footpath as an alternative to continuing northwards to the Roman Wall and the Cheviots.

From Old Ing another green lane, an old packhorse track, leads round the side of Cave Hill to Cam Beck. Two hundred yards/182 m north of Old Ing Farm beside this lane is Dry Laithe Cave, with a 35 ft/10·6 m deep entrance shaft down which a stream falls, to emerge at the large opening of Browgill Cave $\frac{1}{4}$-mile/0·4 km westwards.

The track leads towards Cam Beck and the ravine of Ling Gill. The Gill is a collapsed cave, and great crags reach to a height of nearly 300 ft/91 m, whilst its bed is strewn with blocks and boulders of every size and shape. In midwinter icicles like organ pipes hang from the cliffs and the Gill holds a terrifying silence. In summer it is enchanting; rowans and rock-held hollies catch the sun and ledges are gay with foxgloves, harebells and sheep-bit scabious, and the air is loud with singing birds.

Ling Gill is crossed by a famous bridge, built of grit quarried from the Cam Beck course. It was originally built for the benefit of travellers on the main pre-turnpike road from Settle to Hawes, and a stone tablet records in quaint lettering: 'Anno 1765 (or 68). This bridge was repaired at the charge of the whole West Ridinge.'

From Ling Gill Bridge an easy path leads down the right hand side of the Gill, in places nearly 200 ft/60 m above the stream bed, and even the stream bed itself with its fine waterfall can be followed with care.

From Cam Beck go forward along a mile of rough track to reach a Roman road at Cam End, 1,432 ft/436 m, and bear north over Cam Fell. This Roman road leading to Bainbridge in Wensleydale was once called the Devil's Causeway—a belief that

Dry Laithe Cave, near Horton Ribblesdale

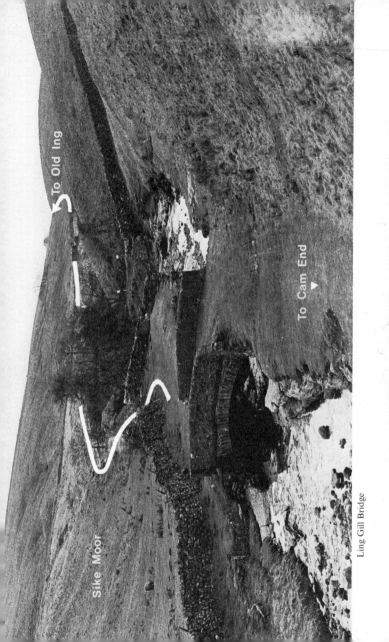

To Old Ing

To Cam End

Sike Moor

Ling Gill Bridge

Gayle and the Duerley Beck, near Hawes, Wensleydale

Great Shunner Fell

Hardrow Force

Footpath to Gayle

Hardrow and Great Shunner Fell from Hawes, Wensleydale

no human hands could have engineered such a road so well, enduring for so long. In the Middle Ages men feared nightfall on the Cam. They hastened onwards, glad to hear the sound of Bainbridge's horn carried to them on the wind. Wolves ranged the tops, and the hornblower sounded the alarm as a warning for all to bring down flocks and herds to safety.

Two miles/3·2 km further along the Roman road the remote farm of Cam Houses appears in a lonely dip. Not far beyond is the watershed of England where the head streams of the Wharfe and Ribble are separated by a patch of hilltop.

We leave the Roman road near Dodd Fell at height 1,877 ft/ 572 m, on an old green track north-easterly alongside Dodd Fell. From this junction there is a marvellous view of hill and dale, and, looking back, the flat top of Ingleborough, 7½ miles/12 km distant.

Our track continues to Hawes over the steep shoulder of Dodd Fell to Ten End, then by footpath to Backsides, Gaudy House and Gayle. The Ten End—Backsides footpath offshoot is not clear, and is difficult to find in mist.

Gayle is an unusual little village, with old stone houses and barns standing higgledy-piggledy in narrow twisting streets. The wide stream which cascades over broad rocky ledges through the village is the home of a considerable floating population of geese, and in dry weather children use the beck as their playground.

Wensleydale

Do not cross the bridge but take the road to Hawes, and after a few hundred yards/metres take the churchyard path on the right-hand side, which delivers you suddenly into the midst of this busy market town (14 miles/22·5 km from Horton; 98 miles/ 157 km from Edale).

Hawes, in Wensleydale, is one of the highest market towns in the country, and is famous for its waterfalls and dairy cheese. Its grey rugged houses and inns huddle round a cobbled main street, which is where the market and sheep sales are held every Tuesday.

Hawes is an ideal place for bed and breakfast accommodation, whether in the good inns or in private houses. It is also a good centre for supplies (early closing day Wednesday) and the next good place for supplies is 4 or 5 days' march away at Alston. The Yorkshire Dales National Park Planning Committee has constructed a new youth hostel in Hawes which is operated on similar lines to those at Crowden and Once Brewed. (This youth hostel is 22 miles/35 km from the hostel at Stainforth, but only 8 miles/12·8 km from Dentdale hostel, although Dentdale is 20 miles/32 km from Stainforth if you follow the Way over Penyghent. Keld hostel is 12 miles/19 km from Hawes along the Pennine Way.)

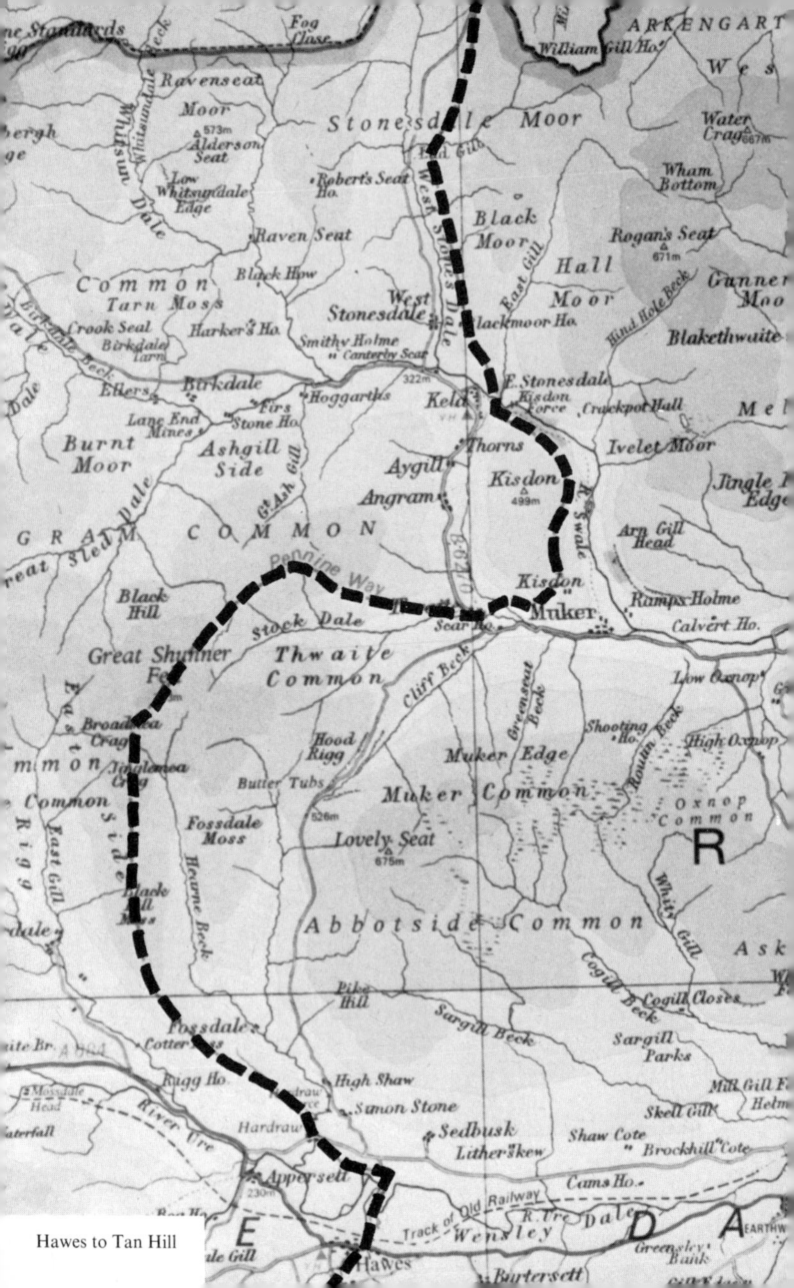

Hawes to Tan Hill

Wensleydale to Swaledale 10miles/16 km

From Hawes take the road to Hardrow, crossing the disused
railway by the station, then north to the bridge over the River
Ure by the riverside pastures. Once across the river keep to the
road for a short distance and up the hill. Above the spinney leave
the road, climb a stile on the left hand side and cross the golf
course by a footpath that leads into the tiny hamlet of Hardrow.

Here a cluster of grey houses stand round a fine old bridge, but
the main attraction is the Hardrow Force, approached through
the parlour of the Green Dragon Inn for a small fee. The walk to
the falls leads up a wooded ravine noted for its acoustic
properties, a place where brass band contests were held in
Victorian days. This tradition has been revived in recent years,
and events cause serious traffic congestion in the valley.

The fall lies at the head of a deep cleft in the hills, plunging
over a projecting shelf of rock in an uninterrupted drop of nearly
100 ft/30 m. The fall is one of the most graceful in the country,
and you can walk behind it and look through it, to see the sun
falling on the silver shower with the glory of a thousand
rainbows. Turner thought it wonderful enough to paint, and
both Wordsworth and Ruskin were captivated by it. That
indefatigable tourist, Doctor Richard Pococke, visited and
described these Wensleydale falls in 1751, and he recorded that in
the great frost of 1739–40 Hardrow Force froze into a single
hollow column measuring $72\frac{3}{4}$ yds/66·5 m in circumference.

Leave Hardrow at the west end of the village and turn north
on a green lane by the school, and follow this old mine track up
the spur of Great Shunner Fell. Shunner is acended by a
footpath following the line of beacons over Black Hill Moss and
Jinglemea Crag, past old coal pits and lead mines. The 2,340 ft/
716 m summit is a long way off, but the route is not difficult to
find even in heavy mist if use is made of careful compass readings
and constant observation of the beacons.

From the summit traverse north-east past a beacon, keeping to

Hardrow Force

To Moor Close Farm and Stock Dale ▲

◄ To Thwaite

B 6270

To Keld ►

Great Shunner Fell, from near Thwaite, Swaledale

Thwaite in Swaledale

Kisdon Hill

Doctor Wood

To Thwaite

Kisdon Hill from Thwaite

Kisdon Force, near Keld, Swaledale

the ridge on the north side of Stock Dale, dropping down to join an old road leading to Thwaite in Swaledale.

Swaledale

Thwaite is a strange little village, where stone houses and walls merge into the landscape, and it was here that the famous brothers Richard and Cherry Kearton were born. The sons of a gamekeeper, they were born naturalists and acquired their intimate knowledge of wild life as boys on these moorlands. Richard was crippled during his early years, and this helped to foster his natural gifts. It was during a shooting party on the moors that Richard attracted the attention of Mr Cassell, the London publisher, and he entered the latter's London office where his wonderful gifts were quickly recognised. Richard won fame as a naturalist and lecturer, while Cherry Kearton, who followed his brother to London, became famous as a pioneer of wild life photography. The two brothers collaborated in many books, and their work revolutionised the study of wild life at close quarters.

Teas are provided at the Kearton Guest House in the village of Thwaite, while the Queens and Farmers Arms in neighbouring Muker, where the Kearton brothers attended school, are able to provide bed and breakfast accommodation. There is a youth hostel at Keld, 3 miles/4·8 km further on our journey.

From Thwaite the Pennine Way climbs up Kisdon Hill, 1,636 ft/499 m, crossing the old corpse track that climbs from Muker by Kisdon Farm. This section of the route over Kisdon presents many difficulties, and problems in misty weather, and is not satisfactorily defined. The signpost in Thwaite village is really misleading, as it directs one to the Muker road. Local people do not admit the officially approved route to be a right of way.

The path crosses the east side of Kisdon Hill, descending to Kisdon Force, where the young Swale tumbles 30 ft/9 m into a rocky glen. The path to Keld village and the youth hostel climbs the bank side again, while the Pennine Way route crosses the Swale by footbridge on its way to Tan Hill.

Keld, 12 miles/19·2 km from Hawes, 110 miles/176 km from

Keld, Swaledale, from the Youth Hostel

Edale, is a fascinating hamlet of grey houses. The youth hostel, above the hamlet on the Kirkby Stephen road, was formerly a shooting lodge, but its austere appearance belies its friendly atmosphere. From the hostel at Keld to the next one at Baldersdale is 15 miles/24 km, a convenient days walk. The alternative is to use bed and breakfast accommodation in Barnard Castle, a few miles/km east of the route, or Middleton in Teesdale 21 miles/33·6 km further on, or to camp.

Keld to Stainmore 10 miles/16 km
Leave Keld and follow the path down to the Swale, and cross by the footbridge to East Stonesdale and Shot Lathe, then by an old road over Stonesdale Moor to the Tan Hill Inn. The track, though indistinct, is well cairned from Lad Gill to Tan Hill.

Tan Hill Inn is undoubtedly the highest licensed house in England. It is situated in an exposed and most desolate spot, 1,732 ft/528 m above sea level. It is dwarfed into insignificance by the loneliness of its surroundings, wild moorland stretching as far as the eye can see in every direction.

The inn was built for the refreshment of miners who lived in bothies or 'shops' near the local workings and returned to their Swaledale homes at the weekends, and also for the carters who carried away the minerals. The coal workings, in shallow seams 4 ft/1·2 m thick, are now no longer worked.

From Tan Hill we leave the Yorkshire Dales National Park and descend north-easterly on a cairned route down Frumming Beck to Sleightholme Beck, and then along a track to Sleightholme Farm. In wet weather avoid Frumming Beck, and instead walk east along the Arkengarthdale road as far as Cocker, and then by a semi-metalled track leading to Sleightholme Farm.

A little beyond Sleightholme take the path which crosses the Beck by a footbridge, and follow a wall leading to Trough Heads Farm, where the Bowes bad-weather route diverges.

The footpath from Trough Heads over Wytham Moor to West Mellwaters is easy to follow, and leads to God's Bridge over the

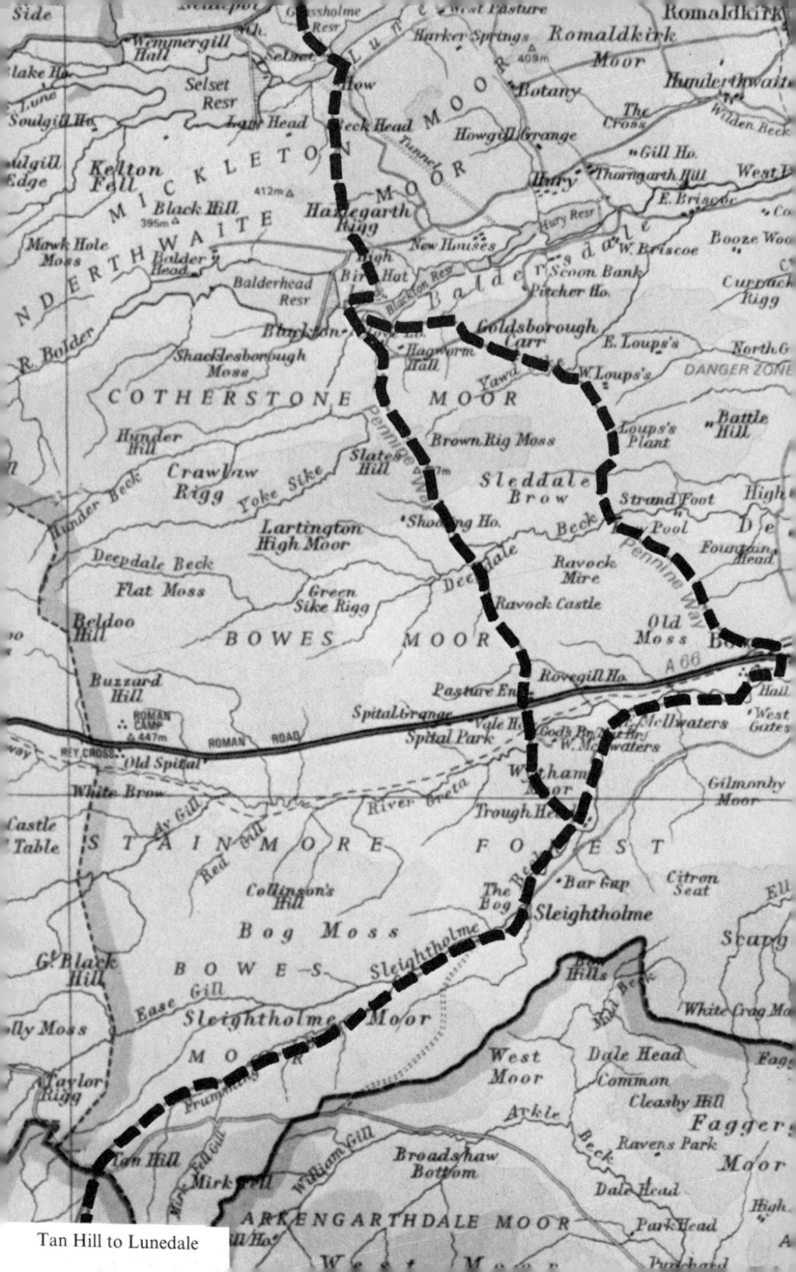

Tan Hill to Lunedale

The Pennine Way near Sleightholme, Stainmore Forest

God's Bridge, spanning the River Greta in Stainmore Gap

River Greta. At this point we are nearly halfway to Scotland, being 120 miles/193 km from Edale. God's Bridge is a curious natural limestone bridge spanning the river, and except at floodtime the Greta flows underground at this point. The river caves under God's Bridge extend to over 3,000 ft/914 m and provide some very sporting and severe caving for experts in the sport.

From God's Bridge pass between the abutments of a demolished railway bridge and follow a rough track which ascends to a gate beside the very busy Bowes-Brough road, route A66.

Alternative Route: Bowes Loop 8 miles/12 km
This diversion is only 3 miles/4·8 km longer than the main Way, yet it avoids the crossing of the Bowes and Cotherstone Moors in bad weather.

From Trough Heads follow the Sleightholme Beck by East Mellwaters and Lady Mires to Bowes. Bowes was one of two Roman forts controlling the Stainmore crossing, but it is today remembered chiefly because Dickens made it the scene of 'Dotheboys Hall' in 'Nicholas Nickleby'. A social conscience inspired Dickens to protest against the bad old Yorkshire schools where boys suffered at the hands of masters such as Whackford Squeers. Much feeling was aroused by this picture, and great improvements resulted.

Dotheboys Hall is now a transport cafe. West End Farm and Clint Farm provide overnight accommodation. To reach the youth hostel at Barnard Castle necessitates 5 miles/8 km of main road walking or an infrequent bus service. The new youth hostel at Baldersdale is 5 miles/8 km further along the way.

Leave Bowes at the western end of the village and pass between the abutments of an old railway bridge on a track which leads north-west to Tute Hill and Levy Pool by Deepdale Beck. Cross Ministry of Defence land by footpaths west of Loup's Plantation to Yawd Sike and Friar House, then west to rejoin the main route at Clove Lodge Farm at the head of Baldersdale Reservoir.

Mickle Fell

Deepdale Beck

Ravock Castle on Bowes Moor

Main Route:
Stainmore to Baldersdale 5 miles/8 km
Stainmore is a vital Pennine crossing and the first major one
since we left the Aire Gap at Gargrave. We leave the main road
at Pasture End and head north beside the enclosure wall west of
the farm, striking out over Bowes Moor to the highest point of
the ridge. Bear north-westerly following the line of cairns to
Ravock Castle, a ruined shepherd's hut. Ahead lies a vast region
of treeless and swampy moorland. The country is deeply indented
and broken by innumerable becks, so that crossing it is not easy,
though much of the ground is good. Flat-topped
Shacklesborough Moss, 1,489 ft/454 m, on Cotherstone Moor is
a good landmark in this featureless country.

Descend to the Deepdale Beck and follow a path north
running parallel to the line of an enclosure wall which is the
western boundary of Ministry of Defence land, and head for a
dip on the horizon. Beyond this dip, at the summit of the next
ridge, stands an old boundary stone known as Race Yate at a
height of 1,402 ft/427 m. It carries the date 1729 and marks the
division of the moors of Bowes and Cotherstone. From this point
there is a gradual descent by height 1,247 ft/338 m on
Cotherstone Moor to the head of Baldersdale at Clove Lodge
Farm. The former Blackton Farm has now been converted into a
youth hostel, conveniently splitting the 30 miles/48 km between
Keld and Langdon Beck into two equal lengths.

The River Balder has been impounded by dams to form
reservoirs for the Tees Valley Water Board, and like those in
neighbouring Lunedale, they add an element of interest to these
bleak little valleys.

Baldersdale to Lunedale 3 miles/4·8 km
Take the track from Clove Lodge and the youth hostel through
Birk Hat to High Birk Hat and the Hunderthwaite road, then by
footpath beside an enclosure wall over Hazelgarth Rigg and
Mickleton Moor to How in Lunedale and the Grassholme
Reservoir.

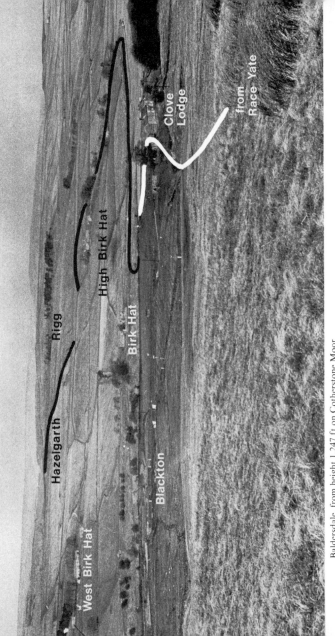

West Birk Hat

Hazelgarth

Rigg

High Birk Hat

Birk Hat

Blackton

Clove Lodge

from Race Yate

Baldersdale, from height 1,247 ft on Cotherstone Moor

Lunedale to Teesdale 3 miles/4·8 km

Cross the bridge over the reservoir and then from beside the first
barn near Grassholme farm make a straight line northwards
through fields to the Mickleton-Brough road, B6276. Cross this
road and beside a barn take the track leading round Wythes Hill,
then turn east on a path crossing several fields above the old
quarries to height 1,577 ft/481 m on Harter Fell. From here
descend gradually north-easterly past two small reservoirs to
reach the road B6277 near a camping and caravan area on the site
of the former Middleton station. Another half mile/0·8 km brings
us into Middleton in Teesdale, 20 miles/32 km from Keld,
130 miles/209 km from Edale. Langdon Beck youth hostel lies
8 miles/12·8 km farther upstream on the River Tees.

Lunedale, from Mickleton Moor

Middleton in Teesdale

Middleton was once the centre of a flourishing lead-mining industry. In 1652 William and Mary granted a charter to the London Lead Company, whose operations were finally abandoned in 1905 owing to the low price of the metal and the decreasing percentage of silver in it, which rendered the business unprofitable. The Quakers who ran the Company looked after their work-people well, providing a school, chapels, a library and substantial cottages. A solid looking stone building with a clock tower, set among tall trees overlooking the little town, was built about 1820 as the head office of the Company; now it is used as an hotel.

The church of St Mary was rebuilt about 1866, and has the only example of a detached belfry in Durham. It is a low structure in the north wall of the churchyard and was built in 1557. Also in the churchyard near the gate are the steps of the old market cross, now supporting a sundial on a round stone shaft; an iron band on the lower step is a relic of the stocks.

In the village is the Bainbridge Memorial Fountain of 1877, an ornamental cast iron canopy with the figure of a child, still much in the 1851 taste.

Teesdale Geology

Both the lead mining which made Middleton important and the scenery which brings visitors to Upper Teesdale are aspects of the earths crust which over wide stretches of this countryside now provide the prominent interest.

The structure of this portion of the Pennines, which extends from Stainmore to the Tyne valley, is comparatively simple. The sharp western slope, along the line through Cross Fell, and reaching more than 2,000 ft/608 m above sea level, forms a great scarp, along a fault which brings the new red sandstone of the Eden valley into contact with the older rocks of the moors. From the steep western escarpment the desolate moorland and bleak

Lunedale to Cauldron Snout

pasture slope gradually away to the east, sinking almost imperceptibly to the plains of the Durham coalfield.

The strange romantic scenery of Upper Teesdale, with its great waterfalls and black scars, is due to the intrusion of igneous rock known as the Whin Sill. The Whin Sill was injected molten into the orderly strata of the carboniferous series and bares itself at Holwick Scars, the crags of Cronkley, Falcon Clints and the gorge of High Cup Nick; it gives the river its most turbulent stretches and forms the two great waterfalls of High Force and Cauldron Snout, and it also forms the crags along the line of the Roman Wall.

Middleton to High Force 4 miles/6·4 km
From Middleton, near the cattle pens just short of the bridge over the Tees, on the Yorkshire (west) side, take a lane leading north-west, which eventually becomes a footpath on the bank of the river.

This riverside footpath is now followed for many miles/ kilometres, and hedgerows and meadows make this a very pleasant walk. Three miles/4·8 km from Middleton we come to Winch Bridge, picturesquely placed amid hazel woods shading a narrow gorge.

This unusual suspension bridge spanning the Tees where it swirls through a ravine was originally built by miners in 1704, and claimed to be the earliest suspension bridge in England. It was composed of two main chains 70 ft/21 m long, with 2 ft/ 0·6 m planks laid across, a handrail only on one side and hung 20 ft/6 m above the river. It was damaged by the great flood of 1771 but was quickly repaired.

Hutchinson in his 'History of Durham' of 1794 says that it was used principally by miners, 'a restless gangway to which few strangers dare trust themselves'. The miners lived in Holwick and worked in the lead mines in the fells above Newbiggin. The bridge collapsed in 1820 while 9 men were crossing, one falling to the narrow rocky gorge below and losing his life. The present structure dates from 1830, and was washed by the river in times of severe flood before the construction of Cow Green reservoir.

The Tees Bridge, Middleton in Teesdale

Winch Bridge near Newbiggin

The Tees at Low Force, above Winch Bridge

Immediately above Winch Bridge the country is more open, and the river comes down over a wide stretch of black basalt in torrents of rusty foam, to form glittering cascades and placid pools. This is Low Force, and the falls are divided by a delightful wooded island called Staple Crag, an upstanding mass of detached rock where gorse and heather grow.

Upstream of Low Force the strange basaltic river bed forms the pleasant cascade of Holwick Force, where the impetuous river flows in deeply cut glen.

We have now been following the Tees for some 4 miles/6·4 km through meadow land and rough pasture, over a large assortment of stiles, along overgrown paths, and past some of the most varied stretches of this ever changing dale. The eroded columns and dykes of Whin Sill which lie across the bed deflect the water into a maze of channels, pools and cataracts, into which the angler casts his fly in search of the brown trout.

If you have kept to the right bank (Yorkshire side) of the river, you don't have to cross the wooden bridge which leads to Holwick Head House. From here we leave the river level and start to climb the high bank over the Tees gorge, on our approach to High Force.

By the gate-way in the fence at the top of this climb is a Pennine Way notice and a map marking the boundary to the Teesdale Nature Reserve.

Six thousand five hundred acres 2 630 ha of Upper Teesdale was declared a National Nature Reserve in September 1963, the second largest in the country. It is bounded on the north by the River Tees and on the south by Mickle Fell, and on the west by the county boundary. North of Dufton Fell it adjoins the 10,000 acres 4 047 ha of the Moor House National Nature Reserve, which the Nature Conservancy Council established in 1952.

The main objects of the reserve are to extend the important researches of highland Britain and those on water conservation which are in progress at Moor House, as well as to safeguard the flora and fauna of Upper Teesdale.

Beyond the gate the path leads through a maze of juniper thickets, and passes very close to the edge of the gorge in several

High Force

High Force

places, giving occasional glimpses of the High Force.

High Force is the finest waterfall in England. The River Tees, after many upland miles of open moor, comes tumbling down a wide rocky channel of Whin Sill, and suddenly leaps 70 ft/21 m into the abyss below, forming a deep swirling pool almost as deep. The vast amphitheatre is bounded by grim walls of black basalt with vertical joints resting on horizontal layers of mountain limestone.

A mighty rock divides the stream in two, though normally the fall on the Durham side is little more than a trickle. At ordinary seasons it is easily possible to scramble on to the top of the central rock, and look down into the chasm below. Even in moderate flow the main fall looks impressive, and on rare occasions of cloudbursts or exceptional floods the central rock is covered, creating an enormous fall 100 ft/30 m high. The thunder of the Force when the Tees is in spate is deafening, and can be heard for a considerable distance.

> Filled was the air with music true
> Though loved, alas! by far too few.
> For nature's sounds are sweet to hear
> If listened for by trained ear.
> The Tees itself, though far away
> Threading its course through distance grey,
> Proclaims aloud with a mighty roll
> Its progress to a far-off goal;
> And rushing madly headlong o'er,
> At High Force leaps with a ceaseless roar.
> Thence bubbling, hissing, onward goes
> Till lost to view in deep repose.
>
> Sir Walter Scott

High Force to Langdon Beck 3 miles/4·8 km
The High Force can also be approached from the Middleton road on the Durham bank, where a footpath descends through the heavily wooded gorge from the High Force Hotel, a discarded shooting lodge of the Dukes of Sutherland. However,

The Tees above High Force

the Pennine Way follows the best approach, on the Yorkshire bank, and visitors also avoid paying the toll to the Raby Estates.

Above the Force the path still continues on the Yorkshire bank, threading its way through a miniature forest of juniper bushes. The juniper is a sturdy, evergreen shrub with thickly spreading branches, and its bluish-green contrasts pleasantly with the changing colours of the bracken. Chips of juniper wood were used for fumigating houses in times of sickness or plague, and the berries are used for flavouring gin.

Opposite the Blea Beck crossing is a whinstone quarry, the ugly stone-crushing machinery striking a jarring note in this wild scene. Further upstream the footpath reaches Skyer Beck. The route then bears north to Cronkley Farm and a bridge over the Tees.

Descending to this bridge we get a glimpse of the bare, treeless fells, the monotony broken by whitewashed farmhouses. The tale is told that a former Lord Barnard had to seek shelter in a farmhouse overnight, and for this kindness he told the farmer to have all the repairs done and the bill sent to his estate agent. When a heavy bill arrived the agent pointed out to a surprised Lord Barnard that the farm was not part of his estate, and consequently his lordship ordered all farms on his estate to be whitewashed annually.

The Tees bridge is crossed and the river followed upstream on the Durham bank, and at the confluence follows the Langdon Beck to the next bridge near New House Farm. At this point the Langdon Beck youth hostel may be easily reached, a distance of 8 miles/12·8 km from Middleton, 138 miles/222 km from Edale.

Langdon Beck Hostel is ideally situated for the next stage of our journey, for from here it is some 15 miles/24 km to the next hostel in the Vale of Eden. This new hostel replaces one on the same site which was destroyed by fire in November 1958. There is excellent accommodation, with hot showers, a drying room and meals provided to take care of the rain-soaked and hungry traveller. Alternatively meals may be obtained from the Langdon Beck Hotel one mile/1·6 km distant.

Upper Teesdale to Vale of Eden 12 miles/19·2 km
From the bridge over the Langdon Beck near New Houses a
footpath leads westerly to Widdybank Farm, though the route is
rather vague.

Widdybank Fell was so named because here an outcrop of soft
slate was once worked for the making of slate pencils, known in
the district as 'Widdies'. Near the farm is an old ruined pencil
mill.

The path now follows Holmwath, the pastures beside the Tees
which are rich in wild flowers. Unique soil and climatic
conditions for alpine plants found here in Upper Teesdale do not
seem to be present anywhere else in the country. Outcrops of
'sugar' limestone weather to give a lime-rich granular soil, and in
such places many of the Teesdale rarities grow. Most abundant
of these flowers are the Stone Violet and the Bird's Eye Primrose,
while Yellow Saxifrage and Shrubby Cinquefoil grow in plenty in
the damp patches beside the river. Much more elusive are the
white Bog Sandwort and the little blue Spring Gentian, but there
are many other more common flowers—violets, primroses and
wild pansies.

The Tees swings round the foot of the high dark cliffs of
Cronkley Scar in a shallow and stony channel, and the scene
increases with magnificence as we approach Falcon Clints along
the path which winds its way on the river bank. Great grey cliffs
rise from a foundation of heather and bilberry tufts, and soon we
are at the junction of the Tees and the Maize Beck—the meeting
place of Yorkshire, Durham and Cumbria.

A few yards/metres away northwards is Cauldron Snout,
where the Tees falls 200 ft/60 m in 150 yds/137 m, the Whin Sill
forming a tremendous series of cataracts. Approaching from
below you turn suddenly to face the stairway of the fall at the
level of the agitated surface of the cauldron. The water pours
into this pool in a white foam over the snout which forms the
final step of the descent, and high above you see its first leap
from the skyline.

It is an easy scramble up the natural rocky stairway on the
eastern bank, from which you can oberve the fall in all its

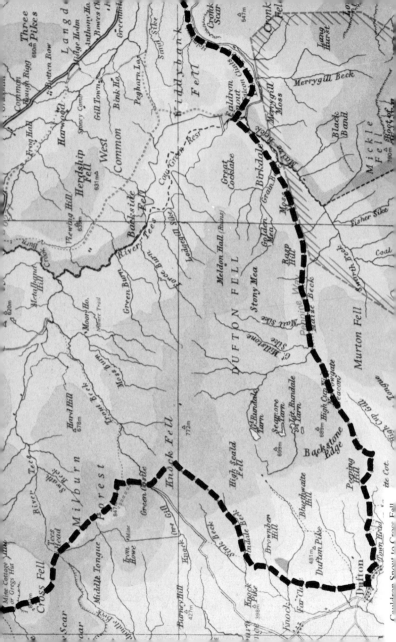
Cauldron Snout to Cross Fell

Falcon Clints

The Tees at Cauldron Snout

grandeur. The view from the top of the fall is the extensive
spread of moorland rimmed by distant fells, whose lower slopes
are possibly dark below white mists that rake their tops.

Above Cauldron Snout the Tees once threaded its way
through a tract of extreme desolation, during which it hardly
seemed to flow, in the long, level expanse of the Weil, but now it
has stopped flowing altogether as it runs into Cow Green
Reservoir. Against a background of amenity value, scientific
study and conservation, proposals to establish a reservoir at Cow
Green excited and stimulated considerable opposition when the
Tees Valley & Cleveland Water Board promoted a Bill in 1967 to
control the abstraction of water from the River Tees primarily to
serve the ICI plant at Billingham. The reservoir was 'opened' on
22nd July, 1971.

At a cost of £2½m 770 acres/311 ha of land have been flooded
to a maximum depth of 75 ft/22 m to contain 9,000 million
gallons/40 914 million litres of water. The 82 ft/25 m high dam.
623 yds/570 m long, dominates the head of Cauldron Snout. The
fate of this fine mountain cataract, and that of High Force,
depend on the volume of water the engineers permit to escape
through the sluices. It is the intention to regulate the flow of the
river at times of high flow, but in dry weather compensation
water will be released to increase normal dry weather flows.

It has been argued that the reservoir will do irreparable
damage to the cause of conservation by flooding an area of
unique botanical interest. Rare plant communities, relics of a
tundra vegetation and considered to be of a unique quality, grow
in this area, and are of importance for long-term biological
research. These plant communities grow on limestone soils
derived from the sugar limestone which lies above the Whin Sill
over this area. Every effort was made to cause the mininum
interference to those parts of the reservoir area, but even so a
small area has been submerged. Recognising the importance of
scientific research in Upper Teesdale, ICI Ltd contributed
£100,000 for study during the ten-year period 1967–1977.

The Dam stands 900 ft/274 m upstream of Cauldron Snout,
and a new footbridge had to be built to accommodate the

Moss Shop

Birkdale

Remote Birkdale Farm on the route from Teesdale to the Vale of Eden

High Cup Nick

Pennine Way, as the original was submerged.

Cross over the fall by the new bridge, and follow the cart track westwards to remote Birkdale Farm, a distance of 5 miles/8 km from Langdon Beck, 143 miles/230 km from Edale.

Beyond Birkdale a path makes for the deserted mine cottage of Moss Shop high up on the hillside, and from there crosses 2 miles/3·2 km of open moor indistinctly, though cairned, among the heather, bent and bog. The hollows in the ground hereabouts are old craters, left by artillery fire from the ranges of Warcop, which occupy the fells on the south side of Maize Beck.

Maize Beck is reached and crossed half a mile/0·8 km further on near a sheepfold, though the stream is impossible to cross at this point when the water is high. If the Beck is in flood keep to the north bank for a further mile/1·6 km until a footbridge is reached spanning a striking gorge, and return to the main path at High Cup Nick. At the Maize Beck crossing by the main path strike across the shoulder of Murton Fell, leaving Maize Beck where it swings northwards, and soon you see the blue serrated outline of the Lakeland fells far away to the west. The path descends slightly then, suddenly, the land falls away at your very feet, and you are standing on the brink of the spectacular and colossal hollow of High Cup Nick.

Shaped like a horse-shoe, the whole of the rim is lined with a series of basaltic columns consisting of small buttresses and gullies. The land falls away sheer and the steep sides below are strewn with black scree. Beyond, the gill broadens into a lovely green plain and the Vale of Eden. High Cup Nick bears all the evidence of erosion by a valley glacier, and it may also have acted as an overflow channel for the Maize Beck lake. The stream that falls gently over the top is certainly too small to account for the extent to which the Nick has been cut.

The summit north of the Nick is Narrowgate Beacon, a name which recalls the days when beacon fires were lit on some of the Pennine tops to give warning of invasion threats and call the countrymen to arms.

A well-defined path leads to the north of the Nick and creeps round the edge of the precipice, and as you advance your attention is divided between the marvels of the cliff and patterned valley far below, and the beauty of the Lakeland panorama.

The path follows the edge of the Nick for over a mile/1·8 km at a fairly constant level, and when the rock buttresses merge with the slopes of the moor, follow a line of cairns which bear away to the right and guide you to a deserted quarry. Upon reaching a ruined limekiln near to a sheepfold, pass through a gate to a grassy track which crosses the slopes of Peeping Hill and gradually descends in a couple of miles/3·2 km to Dufton (7 miles/11·2 km from Birkdale; a total of 150 miles/241 km). Shapely, conical Dufton Pike and Knock Pike are disclosed as you pass through gated pastures down to the road in the village.

Dufton, with its red sandstone and colour-washed houses, is a pleasant village. The cottages are pleasantly arranged round an oblong green which is cut diagonally by the road and ornamented by a well-executed stone fountain. Above the houses can be seen the flat top of Cross Fell, 6 miles/9·2 km away to the north.

Bed and Breakfast accommodation may be available at the village Post Office or some of the cottages in Dufton, while the Stag Inn provides light refreshments. After a long absence a youth hostel has been re-established in the village, and the one at Knock has now been closed. The welcome return of a hostel to Dufton saves an unwelcome detour after a long walk over and across the Pennine watershed.

Cross Fell from the Village Green at Dufton

Dufton to Cross Fell 9 miles/14·4 km
Where the road forks just outside Dufton a narrow track,
becoming a footpath, leads northwards between Knock Pike and
Dufton Pike to the Great Rundale Beck, then an old mine track
leads us to Swindale Beck. The route then follows the stream bed
up on to Green Fell and the summit of Knock Fell, 2,604 ft/
794 m.

In 1952 the Nature Conservancy Council acquired 10,000 acres/
4 047 ha of Knock Fell, Milburn Forest and Dufton Fell for the
Moor House National Nature Reserve. This magnificent site high
in the Pennines is an open-air laboratory for the investigation
of the many problems of the ecology of the British moorlands.

From Knock Fell the route leads north-east of Green
Castle, passing excavations and spoil heaps on the approach to
Great Dun Fell and its radio station at 2,780 ft/847 m. Then
follows Little Dun Fell, 2,761 ft/842 m, and the boggy source of
the River Tees, 8 miles/12·8 km from Dufton and 158 miles/
254 km from Edale.

Climb north-westerly from Tees Head to the summit of Cross
Fell, 2,930 ft/893 m, the highest point in the whole Pennine
range. From the top are magnificent views over the Eden valley
to the mountains of Lakeland, while to the north may be seen the
silver ribbon of Solway, and beyond, Criffel and the hills of
Galloway. Cross Fell was originally named 'Fiends' Fell'.
According to tradition St Augustine erected a cross on its summit.
and thus scattering the devils frequenting it, christened it Cross
Fell.

Cross Fell is most often shrouded in low cloud and bad
weather, and is the source of the Helm Wind. According to the
glossary published by the Meteorological Office of the Air
Ministry, the Helm Wind is a 'violent, cold, easterly wind
blowing down the western slope of the Cross Fell range,
Cumbria. It may occur at all seasons of the year, but mostly
when the general direction of the wind is east or north-east.

Cross Fell · Little Dun Fell · Great Dun Fell

Cross Fell from Milburn Grange

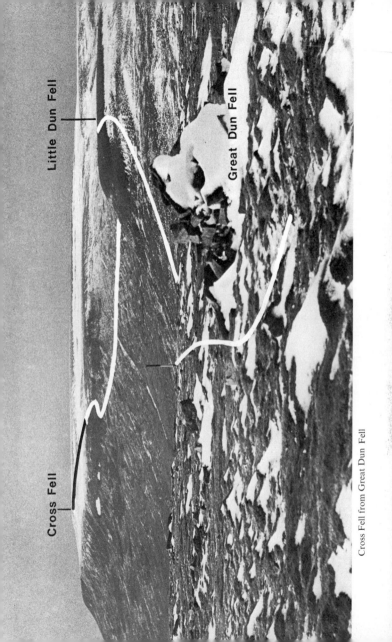

Cross Fell from Great Dun Fell

Great Dun Fell

Summit of Cross Fell, looking south east

When the Helm is blowing a heavy bank of cloud (the Helm Cloud) rests along the range, and at a distance of 3 or 4 miles/4·8 to 6·4 km from the foot of the Fell—approximately along the line of the River Eden—a slender, nearly stationary roll of whirling cloud (the Helm Bar) appears in mid-air and parallel with the Helm Cloud. The cold wind blows strongly down the steep fell sides until it comes nearly under the Bar, when it suddenly ceases. To the west of this calm at the surface, a westerly wind may be experienced for a short distance. The space between the Helm Cloud and the Bar is usually quite clear, although the rest of the sky may be cloudy'.

The Helm is a powerful local wind, caused by cold air pouring down the steep scarp slope into the Eden Valley. The air becomes warmer as it descends, so that whirlpools of rising air are created, and these, rising and condensing, create the Helm Bar. The Helm Wind always stops short of the River Eden, and the contrasts, within a few yards, of its blowing and not blowing are very remarkable. The wind has been known to strip off heavy roofing slates and even uproot turnips from the fields, whilst on the opposite bank of the river one could hold a lighted match without it being blown out.

Cross Fell to Garrigill 7 miles/11·2 km
From the summit of Cross Fell descend by the easy north-west slopes to Cross Fell Well, joining the old corpse road at the western end of the Screes. Should you descend Cross Fell too much to the north your descent will be over rough and tumbled scree. If descending at the east end by traversing the top from the trig point, beware of a dangerous open mine shaft almost in your tracks—not far from Fallow Hill, 2,583 ft/787 m, and a boundary fence.

Follow the old corpse track on its easterly course to Garrigill. This track crosses the fells from Garrigill in South Tynedale to Kirkland in Eden. Coffin bearers no longer used this trail when ground was consecrated in Garrigill, but only after corpses had lain for weeks on the moor in a bad winter.

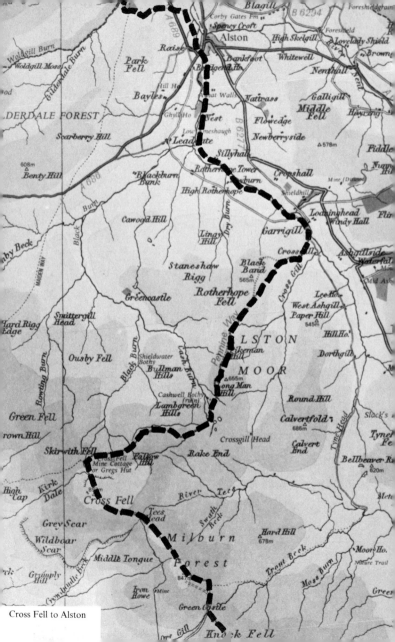

Cross Fell to Alston

Greg's Hut, the bothy on Cross Fell

Across the waste in bygone days,
O'er lonely hills and marshy ways,
There ran a road nor'-west;
Between rough stones on either hand
They carried through that dreary land
The dead men to their rest.

This stony track crosses Skirwith Fell and passes some old
mine workings, where one building has been made into a bothy,
Greg's Hut, a suitable place for shelter, but not too comfortable
to sleep in because of its stone flag floors. The track then leads
over Alston Moor, crossing Pikeman Hill, 2,022 ft/616 m, Black
Band Hill, 1,853 ft/565 m, then steeply down to Garrigill.

This track across Alston Moor is purple with Blue John
crystals, the amethystine or topazine fluorspar generally
believed to exist only at Castleton in Derbyshire. The moor is
rich in ores—zinc blende, barytes, fluospar and galena, the most
important of lead ores.

The Romans discovered lead in the neighbouring fells,
destroying the forest trees for smelting. In the twelfth century
silver and lead were the main attractions, and the Carlisle Lead
Mines, as they were called, were granted the right to cut as much
timber as they desired for smelting purposes.

Up to the time of the 1715 Jacobite Rising, the Alston area
was owned by the Earls of Derwentwater, but after the
participation of the last Earl in the Stuart cause his lands were
confiscated by the Crown and were later granted to Greenwich
Hospital. The Commissioners have remained in possession ever
since, and they still draw revenue from the mining activities, as
well as from the rents of the hill farms. (Of the Earls of
Derwentwater, James was beheaded on Tower Hill on 24th
February, 1716, and his brother Charles on 8th December, 1746,
for their activities in the Jacobite Rebellion.)

In 1750 Greenwich Hospital leased the mines to the London
Lead Company, who worked most of the mines on Alston Moor
until 1905, when the company was wound up. The Company
played a part in Tynedale and Teesdale that affected the whole

life of the valleys. Not only had the lead to be found, mined, smelted and carried away, but the men who did the work had to be housed and provided with at least the necessities of communal life.

Garrigill to Alston 4 miles/6·4 km

Garrigill is a small village at the head of the River South Tyne, lying deep among the dark moors. Garrigill, 7 miles/11·2 km from Cross Fell summit and 165 miles/265 km from Edale, is 15 miles/24 km from the youth hostel at Dufton, and although meals may be obtained from the George and Dragon Hotel by the village square, the next suitable accommodation is at Alston, 4 miles/6·4 km down the valley. The church displays a notice offering shelter, which if accepted should not be abused.

From Garrigill the Pennine Way route continues downstream on the left bank of the River South Tyne. After 2 miles/3·2 km at the crossing of the Little Dry Burn cross the river by a footbridge to Sillyhall, and from here follow the footpath through riverside pastures to the road bridge at Alston, 169 miles/272 km from Edale.

As at Dufton, a youth hostel has been re-established at Alston after a long absence. With the blessing of Cumbria County Council and the Countryside Commission a new purpose-built hostel has been opened on the line of the Pennine Way, built under the same National Parks Act provisions as those at Crowden and Hawes. The next hostel is at Greenhead near Haltwhistle—9 miles/14·4 km from Alston and 7 miles/11·2 km from Once Brewed.

Garrigill in the South Tyne valley

Alston and the Maiden Way to Lambley 10 miles/16 km

Alston is a stone built town, the highest market town in England and a good place for accommodation and supplies. The market cross was erected by Sir William Stephenson, a native of the district who was Lord Mayor of London in 1764.

At Alston cross the South Tyne bridge and continue downstream on a path to Harbut Lodge and the Brampton road, B6292. Follow this road north for 100 yds/91 m, then west to height 1,077 ft/328 m and north-west to the Gilderdale Burn. This section of the route around Harbut Lodge is difficult to follow, and from Alston it may be easier to go by way of Raise, Nether Park and Park Fell to the Maiden Way, following this Roman road northwards to the official route at the Gilderdale Burn crossing.

The Maiden Way is one of the branches of the Ermine Street system, connecting the camps at Kirkby Thore in the Eden valley (which had direct connections with the camps and forts on the west side of the Pennine), with the cross-country road at Stanegate and Hadrian's Wall.

Follow the Maiden Way north again by Whitley Castle and beside a stone wall to the Brampton road at Castle Nook. Whitley Castle Roman Fort measures 150 × 128 yds/137 × 117 m and encloses 9 acres/3·6 ha, and stands on the open hillside commanding a comprehensive view of the South Tyne valley. On three sides there are four ramparts, but on the west, where the fort is overlooked by a ridge of high ground, there are seven ramparts.

From Castle Nook cross the main road and continue on a path, the line of the Maiden Way, through field gates to Kirkhaugh, passing the church which is situated on the opposite bank of the turbulent Tyne. The church has a tall needle-thin spire, and was designed by its vicar without help from an architect, and modelled upon one in the Black Forest in Germany.

Alston, Cumbria, the highest market town in England

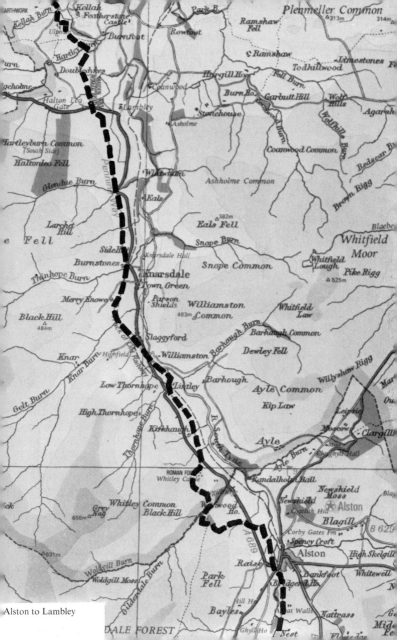

Alston to Lambley

The path continues between the road and railway line to
Lintley, where it crosses the railway, then rejoins the road again
near Slaggyford, 6 miles/9·6 km from Alston, 175 miles/282 km
from Edale. A road leaves the main village street on the left, and
here a track leads right parallel to the railway to the Knar Burn,
crosses under the railway, then by footpath to Merry Knowe and
Burnstones by the Thinhope Burn. Knarsdale lies down the lane
to the right, and in the churchyard is the curious epitaph of one
Robert Baxter, who died on 4th October, 1796:

> All you that please these lines to read,
> It will cause a tender heart to bleed;
> I murdered was upon the fell,
> And by the man I knew full well;
> By bread and butter which he'd laid,
> I, being harmless, was betrayed.
> I hope he will rewarded be,
> That laid that poison there for me.

Pass under the railway arch at Burnstones and bear right of
the farm through fields to the line of the Roman road again,
keeping the stone wall on your right till you reach the pretty
Glendue Burn. Cross the burn by the footbridge and continue on
the heather track of the Maiden Way. On the summit of the hill
by a wire fence cross over a stile, which, although it means
walking in heather, avoids several old fixed gates and very wet
patches on the other side of the fence. At the Pennine Way sign,
recross the fence and follow a grassy track down to the B6292,
4 miles/6·4 km from Slaggyford.

Lambley to Greenhead 7 miles/11·2 km
The route of the Pennine Way over Hartley Burn Common
between Lambley and Greenhead is a complex and not very
rewarding diversion that absorbs a great deal of time and energy.
Although it is doubtful if many people would be willing to tramp
the metalled road, it is recommended that following the line
of the Maiden Way would be a suitable alternative and

timesaver. This would avoid the wall and fence-infested official
route, afford continuous and excellent views of South Tynedale,
and give some sense of purpose by heading along the old Roman
road striking directly at Carvoran and Hadrian's Wall. Opencast
coal workings are predicted in the Lambley-Greenhead area in
the mid-1980s and the Pennine Way will then have to be diverted
temporarily. As the Northumberland County Council have
purchased from British Rail part of the old railway line between
Haltwhistle and Lambley with the intention of making a
footpath along it, there may be the opportunity of providing an
alternative route down the South Tyne valley.

Cross the B6292 near Lambley and keeping a stone wall on your
left pass by old colliery spoil heaps and two barns ahead which
lead us to the Black Burn crossing, then cross the fields north-
westerly towards a prominent two-storey barn and down to the
Hartley Burn. The route now runs upstream for about 300 yds/
275 m then strikes north to reach a fence, which is followed on
the right hand to join a path leading to Batey Shield and on to
the Kellah Burn, where we leave the road at Greenriggs to cross
Hartleyburn Common, past a ruined farmhouse on Wain Rigg
and height 954 ft/289 m on Thirlwall Common.

To the north lie the lonely moors and forests of Spadeadam.
Here ten years ago static firing tests were carried out on the
engines of Blue Streak, Britain's first-stage rocket contribution to
the joint European programme to launch a satellite into space.
Today the site is largely empty, although the Ministry of Defence
still occupy and maintain it, but part of the area is occupied by
the British Gas Corporation for testing oil pipes to destruction,
as part of the research into the technology of North Sea oil and
gas exploitation.

A quarter of a mile/0·4 km south of the Hexham-Carlisle road
A69 at Gap Shield Farm the Pennine Way turns east on a grassy
track by Todholes barn and Tilesheds, then north-west and north
to a village hall beside the main road half a mile/0·8 km west of
Greenhead. Cross the A69 and pass through a wicket gate then
north-easterly across a golf course over height 632 ft/193 m,
dropping down to the golf club house near the Roman road of

Thirlwall Castle

Stanegate. Follow Stanegate east to the Greenhead-Gilsland
road, the railway line and the Tipalt Burn, 7 miles/11·2 km from
Lambley, a total distance of 186 miles/300 km. Here we enter the
Northumberland National Park.

We have now reached the line of Hadrian's Wall, though only
the bare outlines of the Wall and its mile-castles now remain.
Here the Wall passed over a comparatively level tract of land,
and was consequently more exposed to the attacks of the enemy.
Aware of this, the Romans erected a thick line of defence a little
to the south of the Wall, consisting of five camps placed about
half a mile/0·8 km apart.

Many of the farmhouses and outbuildings have Roman stones
built into the walls, while Thirlwall Castle by the Tipalt Burn was
built entirely of Roman masonry. The castle is well seen from the
footbridge as we cross the Tipalt Burn, a tall grey ruin of a tower
with walls 9 ft/2·75 m thick. The youth hostel at Greenhead may
be easily reached by a footpath running between the railway and
the Burn south of the castle.

From the Burn the ditch and vallum of the Roman Wall rise
steeply to the site of Carvoran fort, and the start of our journey
along Hadrian's Wall.

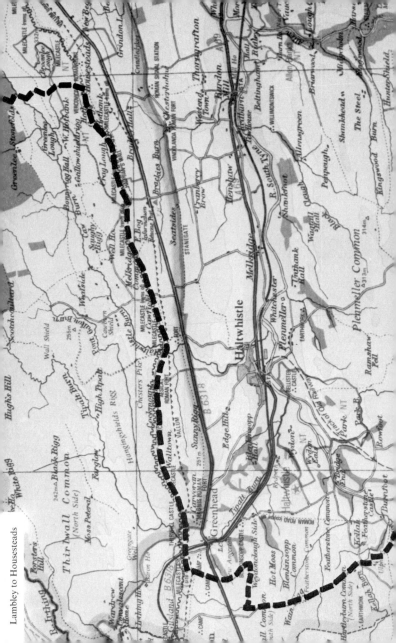

Lambley to Housesteads

The Roman Wall, or Hadrian's Wall, was built about AD 125, and is the largest and probably best known monument of Roman antiquity in Britain. In AD 122 the Emperor Hadrian came to Britain and decided to build a barrier from the Tyne to the Solway to contain the northern tribes, as military panic had shattered the dream of a completely conquered Britain. The work of building the Wall was entrusted to the Legate of Britain, Aulus Platorius Nepos, and within ten years it was complete.

The garrison of the Wall was withdrawn shortly before AD 200 because of civil war on the Continent. The barbarians broke down the barriers, but the Wall was restored by the Emperor Septimus Severus. Then, in AD 383, Magnus Maximus led the British army on to the Continent against Gratian, and the Wall was finally abandoned after 250 years of usefulness.

The Wall extends for 73½ English miles/118 km, or 80 Roman miles, from Wallsend-on-Tyne to Bowness-on-Solway. Though seldom above 6 ft/1·8 m high, even in the best preserved parts, it was once over 15 ft/4·5 m high, the parapet of the rampart wall bringing the total height to 20 ft/6 m. Though 9 ft 6 in/2·9 m thick in places, the average width is 7 ft 6 in/2·2 m, the original and more generous plan being changed while the Wall was under construction.

The Wall
The interior of the Wall consisted of rubble and mortar, and the facing stones were quarried as close behind the Wall as possible. These stones, no larger than a man could carry, are 6–7 inches/15–17 cm high and 10–11 inches/25–28 cm wide, and sometimes extend as much as 20 inches/50 cm into the Wall, tapering inwards in order to bond better. In all, the Wall contained over two million cubic yards/1·5 million cubic metres of material! The Wall was built by the legionaries themselves. Each century acted as an independent working party, building a length of about 50 yds/45 m and then moving on to a similar length elsewhere,

thus the joints between the sections did not always conform.

The Forts

On the Wall were 17 forts, 3–7 miles/4·8–11·2 km apart. The
larger forts, of about 5 acres/2 ha, accommodated 1,000 infantry
or 500 cavalry, while the smaller forts, of 3 acres/1·2 ha held 500
infantry. The forts generally projected beyond the Wall, but on
cliff edges were parallel with it. The walls of the forts were
5 ft/1·5 m thick, and were reinforced by an internal earth bank
derived from a defensive ditch running round the outside. The
internal stone buildings included barracks, a collonaded
headquarters building, the commandant's house, and workshops.
There were also granaries to hold the year's corn supply received
as tribute from the tribes protected by the Wall. Outside each
fort was a spacious suite of baths, various temples and shrines,
and a village for the soldiers' wives and other civilians.

The Milecastles

More regularly spaced were the milecastles, which were normally
separated by a distance of 1,620 yds/1 481 m, a Roman mile.
These were roughly 20 yds/18 m square and held perhaps 50 men
as patrols for sentry duty. Between each pair of milecastles,
about 540 yds/493 m apart, were two turrets, measuring 14 ft/
4·26 m square and holding four men.

The patrolling garrison in the milecastles and turrets must
have consisted of some 5,000 auxiliary troops, while the more
highly trained fighting garrison stationed at the forts numbered
about 14,000.

The Ditch

The Wall was protected on its northern side by a V-shaped Ditch
27 ft/8 m wide and 9 ft/2·75 m deep. The excavated material was
laid to form a broad mound to heighten the ditch and laid on the
south side so as to form no cover for the enemy. The ditch is
always present except where the Wall stands on the edge of a
cliff, and can be followed for miles even in places where the Wall
itself has disappeared.

The Vallum

Running roughly parallel with the Wall on its south side is a much more impressive ditch called the Vallum. It is normally 60–80 yds/54·8–73 m south of the Wall, but runs straight for long distances, to give it a total length of some 60 miles/96·5 km.

The Vallum consists of a ditch 10 ft/3 m deep, 20 ft/6 m wide at the top and 8 ft/2·4 m across the flat bottom. Thirty feet/9 m away on each side of the ditch, and parallel with it, lies a mound 20 ft/6 m wide, formed of the material dug from the ditch. The whole work of the Vallum is thus 120 ft/56·5 m across, and must have taken a million man-days to dig.

The Vallum was the southern boundary of the patrolled military zone along the Wall, and at the same time a customs barrier to civilians. Public entry to the military zone was by unfortified gates controlled from the forts, there being no other access to the Wall at other points.

The Military Way

A Military Way connects the forts, milecastles and turrets, and runs between the Wall and the Vallum. It was a metalled road about 20 ft/6 m wide, and its course can be followed because all the field-gates are placed upon it. Troops could be secretly moved along this road to issue forth at the milecastles or forts in unexpected sallies against the enemy.

The Stanegate

Another Roman road called the Stanegate runs a mile or so south of the Vallum, and connected the main trunk roads to the north. It was built by Julius Agricola, Governor of Britain from about AD 75 to 85, and was used as the main military base-line for Hadrian's new frontier till the decision was reached to move more troops up to the Wall itself.

After the withdrawal of the legions the Military Way and the Stanegate became neglected, and Newcastle was connected with Carlisle by nothing more than a muddy track. In 1745 General Wade's army took 3 days to cover the 22 miles/35·4 km from Newcastle to Hexham, and Carlisle thus fell into the hands of

Prince Charles. As a result a new West Turnpike was constructed in 1751–3, the line between Newcastle and Chollerford being the direct route taken by Hadrian's Wall. The landowners were pleased to sell the useless stone-covered ground beside the Wall, and the fallen material formed a firm foundation.

Along the actual course of the Wall we are often too concerned with features of antiquarian interest to pay attention to the scenery. The Whin Sill ridge which Hadrian's Wall follows for a greater part of its length forms precipitous crags which face northwards across a wild and barren country. The great ice sheet came up against this hard basalt escarpment, to gouge out the softer rocks at the base and leave its aftermath in a series of boggy mosses and basins occupied by lakes or loughs. These loughs, though not very large, gain in impressive dignity by their proximity to the towering dark crags surmounted by the reminders of a long-past military power and discipline.

What is left of the Wall is glorious testimony to the might of ancient Rome. How glorious it is, how great a spell it casts, is known only to those who have wandered along some of its lonely miles in the hills, and with no sound save the wind singing in their ears or a curlew crying in the sedge. No sight in all England is more impressive than the Roman Wall, this thick grey line rolling up hill and down dale as it has done through the centuries, since the days when Christianity itself was young.

The 9-mile/14·4 km length of the Roman Wall is quite clear to
follow though the markings on the older Ordnance Survey maps
are confusing, and the Map of Hadrian's Wall at a scale of
1:31,680 may be more useful.

Carvoran Fort
The fort of Carvoran covers an area of 3½ acres/1·4 ha, but
unhappily it has largely been destroyed by agricultural operations
and all that is left above the surface are a few ploughed-up stones
and the remains of the north-west tower. Some fragments of the
northern rampart remain, and these must have been the ruins
which William Camden found 'very evident' in 1599.

Carvoran is situated on high ground to the south of both
Vallum and Wall and was probably erected before them,
guarding the junction of the Stanegate with the Maiden Way
which comes up to the south-east angle of the station.

The most remarkable discovery of all at Carvoran was made in
1915, just outside the north-east angle of the fort. A postman
delivering letters to the neighbouring farmhouse saw what looked
like an old bucket projecting from the boggy ground. On picking
it up he found that it was a well-made Roman dry measure in
bronze, in perfect condition. The measure bears an inscription
saying that it holds 17½ sextarii (16·8 pints/10 litres). Roman
certified measures are normally quite accurate, though this
measure really holds nearly 20 pints/11 litres, and it is thought
that the inscription was a means of cheating the natives when they
brought their tribute of corn. The bronze measure is the most
remarkable single object exhibited in Chesters Museum.

Carvoran to Walltown Milecastle
Beyond Carvoran cross the Walltown Quarry road, taking the
lane that runs south of the quarry to Walltown Wood.
Immediately after passing through the first cattle grid on this
lane, turn north to where the Wall resumes the basaltic range of

the Whin Sill along the Nine Nicks of Thirlwall. The Nine
Nicks are so named from that number of peaks in the rocky
ridge, though the first four nicks have been removed by quarry
operations.

A fine stretch of Wall runs to Turret 45a, a prominent long-
distance signal tower now in ruins. From here views extend from
Cross Fell and Skiddaw in the south, the broad flash of Solway
in the west, while to the north stretches the moorland waste to
which the eye has become accustomed for many miles.

To the east runs the mighty basaltic ridge. The Wall traverses
this to the top of Walltown Crags and Milecastle 45 (Walltown)
on the top, then descends the steep west side of Walltown Nick.
Walltown Nick is a wide one, and here the ditch reappears to
strengthen the gap. Close behind the Wall, in the middle of the
gap, is a spring surrounded by masonry called 'King Arthur's
Well'. According to tradition this is where Paulinus baptised
King Egbert. In the crevices of the whinstone rock hereabouts
grow abundant patches of chives, said to have been planted by
the Romans.

Walltown to Alloa Lea
Overlooking Walltown Nick is Turret 44b, and then follows
Mucklebank Crag, at 860 ft/262 m the highest peak in the ridge
of the Nine Nicks of Thirlwall. Beyond the eighth nick comes
Turret 44a at the turn on the crest, and the Wall descends into
the ninth and final nick.

The Military Way at this point is very plain to see, and we
soon come to the grassy foundations and rounded southern
corners of Milecastle 44 (Alloa Lea) half hidden by the bracken
of Haltwhistle Common. From Alloa Lea Milecastle the Wall
descends gradually to Cockmount Hill Wood—a fine stretch
exhibiting 6, 7, and even 9 courses of stones in its north face. The
ditch is very irregular, dug sometimes fully, sometimes to half-
width, and often not at all. At the west end of Cockmount Hill
Wood is a circular milestone from the Military Way forming a
gatepost on the line of the Wall.

Great Chesters Fort

To the east we next come to Aesica or Great Chesters Fort,
smaller than either Chesters or Housesteads, but except for the
specialist in Roman history it hardly repays a visit. Aesica
measures 140 × 120 yds/128 × 109 m, and part of the 3 acre/
1·2 ha site is now occupied by farm buildings. The ramparts are
still clearly defined, the west wall being well preserved to a height
of about 5 ft/1·5 m. There are traces of watch towers at the
north-west and south-west corners. In the centre of the fort is a
dilapidated vaulted chamber filled with ferns—the underground
strongroom which lay beneath the Shrine of the Standards.

Excavations in 1939 indicated that Aesica was built during
the construction of the Wall; and also that it was an
afterthought, for a newly built milecastle (No. 43) had to be
demolished to accommodate it. Just outside the east gate was
discovered an inscription describing Hadrian as the father of his
country; this proved the fort to be not earlier than AD 128, when
this title was bestowed on Hadrian.

The water supply to the fort was obtained from the head of
Caw Burn, 2¼ miles/3·6 km away, by means of an aqueduct, now
choked, 3–4 ft/0·9–1·2 m deep and about as wide, which winds
for a distance of about 6 miles/9·6 km to avoid bridges or
embankments.

Visitors to the Black Gate Museum at Newcastle can see the
famous collection of jewellery found in the south gate of Aesica
in 1894. There is a silver chain collar with a pendant, a silver
bangle, a gold ring, a bronze ring set with a gem, and a huge
silver brooch. Above all, there is the famous Aesica Brooch of
gold, a masterpiece of Celtic art, made about the year 100.

From Aesica the Wall bends eastwards at Turret 42b. From
here the ditch is boldly developed, but the Wall is for the most
part traceable only by the ruins on its foundations. Just before
Burnhead Farm pass through a gate to the north side of the Wall
and to the crossing at the Haltwhistle Burn.

Just below this crossing a large Roman watermill was
excavated in 1908. Part of the undershot wooden mill-wheel was
found, and the big mill-stones are exhibited in Chesters Museum.

The mill is now buried by quarry spoil, and Turret 42a nearby has been destroyed by quarrying.

Haltwhistle Burn Camps

Around this area are a remarkable group of temporary camps, thought to have sheltered men building the Wall. A little to the south of the Wall where the Carlisle road crosses the Haltwhistle Burn can be seen the deep grass-covered ditches of Haltwhistle Burn Fort. The fort appears to have been added to the Stanegate early in Hadrian's reign to guard the stream crossing. This was at a time when it had been decided to build the Wall, but while it was still intended to keep the main military concentration on the Stanegate. When the Wall was built the fort was demolished, and was partly buried beneath the refuse of a Roman quarry.

Two miles to the south lies Haltwhistle, a quiet little industrial town pleasantly situated amid beautiful scenery near the River South Tyne. Bed and breakfast accommodation is available at the Red Lion and Manor House hotels, but if lodging has been found near Greenhead it will not be too far to continue eastwards along the Wall to the youth hostel at Once Brewed.

Cawfields

Back to the line of the Wall again follow the track at the foot of the quarry to Hole Gap, where the Wall follows Cawfields Crags. The old quarry has been made into a picnic site with car park and toilets. The tarmacadam track is the official route, leading towards Cawfields Farm, but the path beside the quarry pond is more attractive. Leave the quarry foot and climb a track to a gate in the fence, turning left to the renovated Milecastle 42 (Cawfields). The milecastle measures internally 63 × 49 ft/19·2 × 14·9 m, and its 8 ft/2·4 m thick walls are 7 to 8 courses of masonry high. The gateways, both on the northern and southern sides, are of large dimensions, and the pivot holes may still be seen. It is difficult to speculate why this milecastle should differ from the rest in having a gateway to the north, as it opens directly on to the edge of the crag, which is precipitous.

Opposite Cawfields Milecastle the Vallum is in a state of

preservation hardly equalled in any other part of its course, where it runs uninterrupted in a straight line for almost 5 miles/ 8 km. The planning of the Military Way is also interesting. It crosses the north mound of the Vallum, travels for 250 yds/228 m along the north berm, and then recrosses the mound. The position of the Vallum left no room for the road, although had the road been contemplated when the Vallum was laid out, nothing would have been easier than to place the Vallum a little more to the south. The road is thus later in the frontier scheme than either Wall or Vallum.

Cawfields Crags to Winshields Crags

The Wall is in an excellent state over Cawfields Crags to Turret 41b, but afterwards is for some distance nearly uprooted. Pass Thorny Doors and Bloody Gap, then the site of Turret 41a, gently dropping down into Caw Gap. Opposite the turret the ditch reappears, though only for a few yards. A road passes through Caw Gap, where the Wall, as usual, bends to the south on either side, so as to protect the line of attack. To the north of the gap is a lonely farmhouse called Burn Deviot, formerly the resort of smugglers and sheep-stealers, and now inhabited, it is alleged, by the spirits of the persons murdered there. Two large stones to the south of the gap near the Carlisle road are called the Mare and Foal, and are probably the remains of a Druid circle.

The next broad depression is Boggle Hole Gap, and a gentle ascent brings us to Milecastle 41 (Melkridge), 1,641 yds/1 500 m east of Cawfields Milecastle. Next comes the ridge itself and Turret 40b, and the deep valley of Lowdham Slacks, where the Wall acquires its ditch again.

The Wall then ascends Winshields Crags, attaining an elevation of 1,230 ft/345 m, the highest point throughout its course. A wide and magnificent view extends from Scotland to Cross Fell. Here a fine piece of the Wall is preserved by the Department of the Environment. An 8 ft/2·4 m wall stands on a foundation 10 ft/3 m wide; the foundations had already been laid when a change of plan reduced the width, though the north face remains unbroken.

Winshields Crags to Peel Crags

The Wall descends the basalt ridge and passes the remains of
Milecastle 40 (Winshields), which has walls uniformly 6 ft 9 in/
2 m thick. The distance between this milecastle and milecastles 41
adn 39 are exceptionally long, measuring 1,850 and 1,806 yds/
1 691 and 1 651 m respectively, when the usual measurement was
as close to 1,620 yds/1 481 m as possible.

Beyond Winshields Milecastle the ditch begins again, and
continues as far as the gap at Steel Rigg. Steel Rigg is a good
spot from which to leave the Wall if accommodation for the
night is required—either at the inn of Twice Brewed or the youth
hostel at Once Brewed, half a mile/0·8 km south on the Carlisle
road.

The new inn of Twice Brewed replaces a famous coaching inn
of the same name, and good meals may be obtained there on
request. Further to the east and immediately south of Peel Gap
at a crossroads is the Once Brewed Youth Hostel. The original
hostel was acquired in 1934 and occupied former farm buildings,
but accommodation was limited and a new hostel was built
alongside. It was opened in Easter, 1968. Alongside the youth
hostel is an information centre with toilets and car park. The
centre contains a display of material relating to the
Northumberland National Park, including photographs, relief
model and large-scale plan of the Hadrian's Wall area. It is 14
miles/22·5 km from Once Brewed to the next youth hostel at
Bellingham.

Diversion to Chesterholme

Once Brewed is perhaps the best place to mention the camp at
Chesterholme, the Roman Vindolanda, some 2 miles/3·2 km east
down the course of the Brackie's Burn, and standing alongside
the line of Agricola's original road, the Stanegate. The camp
covers $3\frac{1}{2}$ acres/1·4 ha and is under the guardianship of the
Department of the Environment, and of particular interest is a
Roman milestone, beside Brackie's Burn and Stanegate.
Uninscribed and nearly 6 ft/1·8 m high, the milestone has the
distinction of being the only one in Britain in its original position.

A section of the Wall has been constructed in stone and in turf, to show its original height, and there is also an excellent museum.

Steel Rigg to Crag Lough

However, our interest lies mainly along the line of the Wall, and we return to the basalt ridge at Steel Rigg, where there is a car park and toilets. A fine stretch of Wall runs eastward from the road, and the section of Wall from Steel Rigg to Housesteads is under the care of the National Trust. Where the Wall descends a steep cliff into Peel Gap, an obviously weak point in the defence, the Wall bends to the south, then to the east, then to the north again, thus enclosing the valley on three sides.

The Wall runs steeply up the side and along the edge of Peel Crag where tall and precipitous basaltic columns cling to the side of the steep drop to the north. Here the Wall is in fine condition, with Turret 39a in its south face. The cutting and embankment of the Military Way south of the turret are well worth viewing.

After Turret 39a is another depression known as Cat's Stairs, offering a precarious route to the bottom of the crag. Further east is another depression into Castle Nick where there are the remains of a well-preserved milecastle—Milecastle 39 (Peel).

Peel Milecastle measures some 50 ft/15 m from east to west and 62 ft/18·8 m from north to south. The side walls are 7 ft/2·1 m thick and have 6 or 7 courses still standing. At the northwest corner are the remains of a small barrack building, and foundations of other apartments still remain. South of Castle Nick the Military Way appears in very perfect condition, with kerbstones complete on each side. Its course can be followed because the well-drained foundations permit finer grass to grow upon it than elsewhere.

The Wall rises steeply from Castle Nick and runs along the verge of the cliff, then sharply turns to the south and descends into Steel Rigg Gap, where the Wall stones are stepped horizontally into the face of the ground. Now the Wall clings to the very edge of the precipice of High Shields Crag and passes through a little copse, affording occasional pleasant views of Crag Lough and Hotbank Crags beyond.

Hotbank Crags   Highshield Crags   Peel Crags

Hadrian's Wall follows the Whin Sill crags

Hotbank
Crags

Highshield Crags

Crag Lough

Milecastle 39

Hadrian's Wall, looking east from Castle Nick

Hotbank Farm from Crag Lough

Winshields Crags

Peel Crags

Highshield Crags

Retrospect from Hotbank Crags

Sewingshields Crags

Housesteads Milecastle

Hadrian's Wall from Cuddy's Crags

The Wall descends into Milking Gap, and is again accompanied by the ditch, and then bends at a sharp angle to take the ascent of Hotbank Crags.

Crag Lough is a shallow little mere, darkened by the reflection of the black basalt cliffs rising 200 ft/60 m sheer from the water. The eastern end and northern shores are bounded by marshy ground with natural thickets of willow, and among the reeds moorhens, swans and wild duck make their nests. Here may be found different species of pond weed, the yellow water lily, the reed mace and other botanical specimens. In the crevices of the crag rowans, cling, and mountain parsley fern and saxifrage grow.

South of Milking Gap the broad shoulder of Barcombe Hill rises above Chesterholme camp, with a magnificent view from the Long Stone on its summit of the Roman Wall stretching from the Nine Nicks of Thirlwall to Sewingshields Crags.

Hotbank to Housesteads
In Milking Gap pass through a gateway in the Wall, and follow the course of the Wall on its south side as it ascends from Hotbank Farm. Opposite Hotbank Farm are the turf-covered remains of Milecastle 38 (Hotbank). This was partly excavated in 1935 and an inscribed stone was found, recalling its building by the Second Legion under Aulus Platorius Nepos, who was the Governor of Britain from AD 122 to 126.

The Wall climbs the hill to Hotbank Crags, with its fine views of the Northumberland lakes. The largest is the beautiful Greenlee Lough, north of the Crags. This is one of the places where the white water-lily grows wild, and in autumn and winter is the haunt of scores of swans. To the east stretches the lovely expanse of Broomlee Lough. Looking back the way we have come, Crag Lough and the mighty Whin Sill crags form a picture of impressive grandeur, the black crags rising thickly wooded above the sombre lake, and the sheer bare cliffs receding into the distance.

The Wall runs splendidly along the cliffs, and in many places is in excellent condition. This sector is cared for by the National Trust, which has built up the south face of the Wall, though the

Housesteads Milecastle

north face is still in disrepair, and the remains of Turrets 37a and 37b are buried. To the east the Wall disappears for a time and it is best to walk along the Military Way to the site of Turret 37a in the steep defile of Rapishaw Gap, a favourite pass for moss-troopers. A drovers' road leads northwards on to the wild moors beyond Greenlee Lough. This is the route of the Pennine Way on the next stage through Wark Forest to Bellingham, and we return to this point when we have visited Housesteads Fort.

Housesteads Milecastle

From Rapishaw Gap the Wall ascends Cuddy's Crags, with the most celebrated view of the Wall surging up and down the rocky heights. The Wall dips then rises again to Milecastle 37 (Housesteads), the finest example of these structures now to be seen. The Milecastle is of a pattern closely resembling that at Cawfields, and was built by the same legion. It meaures 50 × 60 ft/15 × 18 m, and the north wall stands 14 courses or 9 ft 6 ins/2·89 m high. There are some excellent photographs of excavations made in 1933 exhibited in Housesteads Museum.

Housesteads Fort

Housesteads is the finest and best preserved of all the 17 forts that housed the auxiliary regiments on Hadrian's Wall. The fort measure 610 × 367 ft/186 × 111 m, covers an area of 5 acres/ 2 ha, and is set in a fine commanding spot on the edge of the basalt cliff. The ruins are extensive and perfect, the bad reputation of the district due to the activities of moss-troopers saving the fort from destruction. These horse-stealers and plunderers raided the neighbouring countryside, and many pele-towers and fortified houses still exist to remain as evidence of their activities. It was not until the early 1700's that the last moss-troopers ceased to hold Housesteads as their den.

The entrance to the fort is through the south gateway, paying a small charge to the custodian for the privilege. This is also the main entrance used by visitors who have left their vehicles by the Carlisle road, and have climbed the hill to the fort past the remains of the civil settlement.

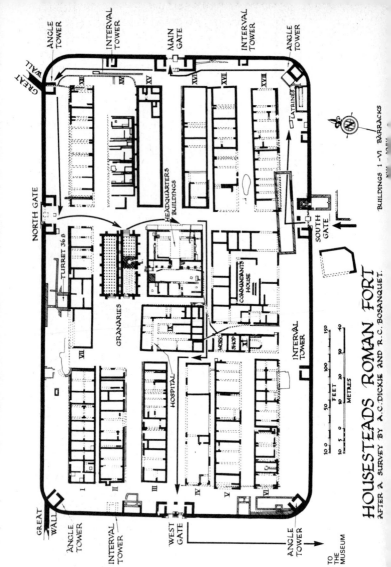

A tour of Housesteads Fort

Housesteads Fort: The Latrines

The South Gate

Entering Housesteads by the South Gate into the Via Praetoria, we are struck by the massive masonry remaining, the south wall standing 10 or 12 courses high. The north and south gates are nearer to the east side of the fort than the west, so the main streets cut the fort into four unequal parts.

The guardchambers of the gateway are still there on both sides, but that on the east was occupied by some moss-troopers who added a tower outside the Wall and built a lime-kiln inside. The pivot-holes for the gates are still visible, and so are the marks of chariot wheels on the flag stones. The Via Praetoria running north is not in its original state, and at some time a building was erected across it just inside the gateway.

The Latrines

Following the inside of the fort wall to the east, we come in the south-east corner to the latrines. This is an oblong building with a central paved walk bordered by channels, once excavated but now covered, around which runs a deep sewer that was once covered by seats for which a few dowel holes remain. There is a large stone trough inside the latrines which was probably used for washing clothes.

Near the latrines, behind the south-east angle tower, is the best preserved water tank in the fort, once fed by a spout from the flat roof of the tower. The large stone slabs which form its sides are jointed with lead, and bound together with iron straps set in lead. The inner face of the slabs accommodates iron hold-fasts set in lead, which held a vanished lead lining in position. Outlet holes at different levels fed a stone channel at ground level for flushing the latrine system. The top edges of the tank are much worn, having been used by the soldiers for sharpening their weapons.

The fort appears to have had no wells inside it, and evidently all the rainwater from the roofs of the buildings was collected and used. The gutters for leading water to various points have been discovered, and the whole drainage system illustrates the care devoted by the Roman army to matters of hygiene affecting the health of their troops.

The East Gate

Turn left up the hill to the East Gate, the main entrance to the fort from the Military Way. The eastern wall, which is 5 ft/1·5 m thick has been cleared of the earthen rampart which enabled the soldiers to man the defences, and the massive masonry can be closely examined.

The East Gate consists of two portals. The south portal was blocked up in the second century, while the threshold of the north portal still exhibits the holes in which the pivots moved, the stones against which the gates stuck when they were closed, and the 8 in/20 cm deep ruts caused by the chariot wheels. These grooves are 4 ft 8½ ins/143·5 cm apart, the modern British Railway gauge. The story, however, that this gauge was based upon them is without foundation. George Stephenson determined the dimension, some years before the gateway was discovered, on the instruction of Howard Pease, by averaging the measurements of 100 country carts. It is coincidence that the wheel gauge of Roman carts approximated to that found convenient ever since.

From this gateway to the opposite one in the west ran the main street, or Via Principalis. Immediately west of the East Gate are seen the remains of a long building of very solid masonry, furnished with a small set of baths at its east end. This appears to be a range set apart for social uses, as opposed to the normal barrack or stable block.

Proceeding northwards along the inside of the east wall we come to a converted interval tower, one of several to be seen around the walls. The tower has been strengthened by a solid platform of masonry for holding a catapult or ballista, and past this we continue to the North-East tower where the Wall joins the fort.

The North-East Tower

The North-East angle tower of the fort seems to have been moved after the Wall was built, an indication that the fort was built before the Wall. From here there is a good view of the Wall leading down to the Knag Burn and up to King's Hill and Sewingshields Crag.

Housesteads Fort: The Granary

The Knag Burn

Below in the dip lies the Knag Burn Gate where there was a customs barrier, a gateway facilitating trade with the civil settlement of the fort and the tribesmen to the north. The gateway was flanked by guardchambers and closed by door both at back and front, enabling a careful check to be made of those who were permitted to cross the frontier. Nearby the Knag Burn runs under the Wall in a remarkable culvert, still covered with slabs and paved at the bottom.

The North Gate

Follow the northern wall of the fort to the North Gate. The gateway appears to lead into space, but it had a roadway ramp leading up to it, though this was removed to reveal the interesting foundations to better advantage. The North Gate is beautifully built and still massive in ruins, the outside of the north rampart wall being one of the finest pieces of masonry on the line of the Wall.

From the North Gate to the centre of the fort we follow the Via Praetoria. On the east side of this street is a very large building, 147 ft/44·8 m long and 30 ft/9 m wide. At its eastern end are several small chambers, one of them having been heated by flues beneath the floor, and another containing a cistern or bath. On the west side of the street are two large apartments— one 78 ft/23·7 m long and 18 ft/5·4 m wide, the other not quite so long, having at its western end a moss-trooper's kiln for drying corn. Some of these large buildings were doubtless the halls in which the public business of the district was transacted, and others were used as the residence of the prefect and his chief officers. The foundation walls of many other chambers, inhabited chiefly by the ordinary soldiers, remain, but there is little to indicate the internal arrangements of them.

The Granaries

Just south of the North Gate are two great granaries, the southern one containing a moss-trooper's corn-drying kiln. The northern granary clearly exhibits ventilators in the walls and a

Housesteads Fort: The West Gate

forest of short stone pillars which supported the wooden floor
joists. In the southern wall socket holes where the beams rested
to support the floor are still visible. The purpose of this raised
floor, with ventilation below it, was to keep the stored corn cool
and dry, while the external buttresses reinforced the outer wall,
cut by the ventilators, against the weight of piled wheat. Between
the central walls of the granaries is a row of pillars, and it is
thought that originally these supported the roof, but maybe after
the original building was demolished it was found easier to divide
the granary into two by means of the centre walls. The buildings
were entered from the west, where the wide thresholds of their
great double doors are to be seen.

The Headquarters Building

A few yards below the granaries is the Principia, or Headquarters
Building, at the junction of the Via Principalis and Via Praetoria.
Little is left of the foundations, but sufficient to show the general
plan. At the entrance were fine reliefs of Mars and Victory, and
these are now in the Chesters Museum. The front courtyard had
a verandah supported on columns, and was later walled off into
rooms. The column bases can still be seen. From the courtyard
an archway led into the Cross Hall. In this was the seat of justice,
and the remains of the dais can be seen in the north-west corner.
From this hall there were the usual five openings into the Shrine
of the Standards and the Regimental Offices. In a room beside
the Shrine were found over 800 arrow heads with traces of their
wooden shafts still sticking to them. They are now on display at
Chesters Museum.

The Commandant's House

The Commandant's House stood to the south of the Principia,
but very little of it is left uncovered. Westwards are more barrack
buildings and the remains of the hospital, but they have not been
completely excavated.

The West Gate

We now come to the West Gate, the finest and most complete of

all the gateways to the fort, eleven courses of masonry high. At
some period following its erection the northern portal of the
outside gate and the southern portal of the inside gate were
blocked up, thus making the entrance passage a diagonal one.
The threshold has been worn by the tread of feet, and many
projecting stones in the outside wall have been rounded and
hollowed by the soldiers sharpening their weapons upon them.
The pivot holes for the doors are well seen, and also for the bar
which fastens them. The locking device is an inverted 'L' shaped
groove into which the bar was slid, the other end fitting into a
hole in the opposite wall. The doors themselves were about 5
inches/12·7 cm thick.

Housesteads Museum
Outside the West Gate turn left down the hill towards the
Museum, outside the southwest angle of the fort. The museum
does not contain many of the treasures of Housesteads, these
being at Chesters Museum and some at the Black Gate Museum
in Newcastle. However, it contains a very good model of the fort
as it was in Roman times, and models of the West Gate and one
of the buildings in the civil settlement. There are detailed plans
and photographs of some of the buildings and early excavation
works.

Hadrian's Wall to Wark Forest 2 miles/3·2 km

Leaving Housesteads now we can return to the Pennine Way by
crossing the fields westwards along the line of the Military Way
for ½-mile/0·8 km to Rapishaw Gap. Before passing through the
gateway we can take a look to the south, and catch a quick
glimpse of the rolling Pennine massif, high, bare, and
uncompromising. The landscape to the north to which we now
turn is not so different to that of Roman times, despite the
skyline becoming marred by the conifers of the Forestry
Commission.

Over the wild and open moors the moss-troopers raided and
rustled each other's cattle and sheep. No more are these fells wild
and open, for the Forestry Commission have covered them with
the largest forests in Britain, stretching from the Roman Wall to
the Cheviots themselves, and this has swept all the sheep off the
fells and closed and left derelict numerous farmhouses. It was as
though the hills had been enveloped in a green cloud, where each
fell top has lost its individual character and streams have been
spirited away among the relentless smoothing tide of trees.

Not only do these vast plantations of the Forestry Commission
indicate a change of topography. On this, the Pictish side of the
wall, the valleys lie in great concave basins between narrow
ridges, whence the eye ranges mile after mile over great stretches
of country to the next ridge that jags the skyline. On the southern
side of the Wall narrow valleys cleave great convex moorlands,
so that views are limited either to the tops of the moors or the
narrow limits of the valley.

The Pennine Way crosses the wall and goes due north on an
old drove road to a ruined lime kiln, then continues over a piece
of somewhat boggy ground, crossing Jenkins Burn and passing
between Broomlee and Greenlee Loughs.

The moors to the north put the Roman Wall itself in a proper
perspective. Looking back, we can see that the few courses of
stone crowning the Whin Sill soon melt into the distant

Housesteads to Bellingham

panorama of moorland. Only the heights around remain—or did so until the Forestry Commission got to work and began to change the untamed face of Northumberland.

The track passes the ruins of Crag End, and crosses over to a farm gate just past East Stonefolds Farm.

The track has been easy to follow and as it mounts the slopes beyond Stonefolds it is still well defined as it leads towards Haughtongreen. But here the forest zone is reached, and foresters, however well meaning they may be, seem to have a habit of upsetting even the best of tracks. Not that there is any lack of paths through the trees. Indeed, their very multiplicity is puzzling, so much so that it becomes difficult to separate fire-ride from authentic track.

A track leads northwards through the forest to emerge at Middleburn, but this is not the one we want: the track we need to follow emerges a little to the west of Ladyhill, and it is easy to follow provided that in the forest you follow the line of the telegraph wires.

Black Dike
From Stonefolds continue generally northwards on the forest road and after about 1 mile/1·6 km fork right on a path to emerge at a gate opening out on to Hawkside Fell. The eastern boundary of the forest follows the line of the Black Dike, an ancient cutting and earthwork of unknown antiquity, supposed to be the boundary line between the kingdoms of Northumbria and Cumbria. It can be traced in places from the North Tyne (at High Cariteth near Tarset) to the South Tyne (at Moralee between Haydon Bridge and Bardon Mill). It cannot be seen on boggy ground, but elsewhere may be noticed as a ditch 14 ft/ 4·2 m across and 4–6 ft/1·2–1·8 m deep; the excavated earth forms a mound on the east side, indicating that the area cut off was to the east of the Dike in the fork of the two Tynes.

Kimmin's Cross
The crossing of Haughton Common is not very easy going, but from 1,078 ft/329 m on Hawk Side bear east on a green track

Hawk Side

Retrospect from Kimmin's Cross

towards the foundations of Kimmin's Cross, on the south edge
of the forest beside a gate bearing a fire warning sign. (Kimmin's
Cross is now correctly marked on the 1:50,000 scale maps, but is
spelt Comyn's Cross; all now remaining is a pile of stones.)
According to legend Cumming (or Kimmin), a northern
chieftain, was slain on this spot by the jealous sons of King
Arthur after he had paid a visit to the King at his castle near
Sewingshields.

From Kimmin's Cross we re-enter the forest, and descend by
forest rides generally northwards through the plantations to
emerge on a lane just west of Ladyhill, a distance of 6 miles/
9·6 km from Housesteads, 201 miles/323 km from Edale.
Opposite Ladyhill a Pennine Way sign points northwards, and a
track leads north-easterly skirting the forest, crossing Fawlee
Sike and leading to the Warks Burn.

Warks Burn to Bellingham 5 miles/8 km
Across the Warks Burn the route becomes easier to follow. A
footpath leads past Horneystead to Ash and a track continues to
the road, where turn to the right and then turn off left at
Leadgate Cottage by green track to Low Stead and Linacres by
the Blacka Burn. From Low Stead turn east to the road, turn
north to the road junction, where a footpath descends to the wild
and rapid Houxty Burn and a footbridge to Shitlington Hall.

Shitlington Hall is written in old documents as Shotlyngton
Hall, and this house superseded the old manor house of a branch
of the Charlton family. In 1528 it was recorded that a band of
Border thieves, led by 'Willie o' Shotlyngton' and others, raided
neighbouring Wolsingham, robbing many houses and carrying
off the priest of Muggleswick as prisoner. William Charlton was
killed in the pursuit which followed, and his body afterwards
hung in chains in Hexham.

Keep Shitlington Hall on your left hand and go straight on
and bear to the right of a group of farm buildings, through a
wicket gate, and by footpath leading over to Shitlington Crags,
through another wicket gate in a wall and to the top of
Ealingham Rigg.

The Warks Burn

Bellingham

Bellingham lies down below by the banks of the North Tyne, and the route leads down from Ealingham Rigg to the road B6320 via Fell End, giving a mile of road walking into the township. It seems that the old footpath leading in a direct line to the Army School Camps at Brown Rigg has fallen into disuse, but as there is a new footbridge over the Eals Burn this alternative would save some time at the end of the day.

A picturesque stone bridge built in 1835 crosses the Tyne and we enter Bellingham, 6 miles/9·6 km from Ladyhill and 207 miles/333 km from Edale. Bellingham is a plain little market town in beautiful surroundings. The architecture is dull and uninviting, perhaps still in the tradition of the turbulent old times, when the less attractive a town was the fewer temptations it offered to the lawless inhabitants of the Borderland.

Being in the direct route of the moss-troopers of Tynedale, Redesdale and Liddesdale, when riding south on their too frequent forays, it is not to be wondered that there are no traces of medieval grace or Jacobean elegance in this ancient town. From some valuable old records it appears that the name was formerly written Bellinjham, thus confirming the local pronunciation, Bellinjum.

There are some splendid old houses not far from the river, and we pass one of them, Lee Hall, on our way into the town. The house is a delightful early eighteenth century building mentioned as the probable scene of the tragical incident narrated by the Ettrick Shepherd in his 'Tale of the Long Pack', more of which will be related later. Here also was a healing spring where the lady of the hall used to dip rickety children before sunrise. After sunset on the same day they were again dipped, but in the Tyne, and their clothes were thrown into the water; if the clothes floated, so the story runs, the owner's rickets disappeared.

Half hidden among the houses is St Cuthbert's, a church of considerable interest, built about the year 1200. The church has a massive stone roof, consisting of hexagonal ribs about 3 ft/0·9 m apart, overlaid with heavy grey stone slabs. Only one other church in England (that at Barton in Cumbria) has a complete

Ladyhill

Linacres

Ash

Shillington Hall

Retrospect from Ealingham Rigg

Blakelaw

Callerhues Crag

Hareshaw House

Hareshaw Dene

Brown Rigg Camps

Bellingham from Ealingham Rigg

The Long Pack, St Cuthbert's churchyard, Bellingham

stone roof integral with the rest of the building: at Bellingham the ribs of the ceiling vault actually merge into the walls.

The necessity of such a ponderous structure will be evident when it is remembered that, according to tradition, the chancel (which has had a wooden roof) was twice burnt by the Scots during the Border wars. Another illustration of the unsettled condition of the country in olden times is seen in the extremely narrow windows of the nave, widely splayed inside, which could be made available for defence purposes. The thick nave walls were heavily buttressed in the eighteenth century when they were beginning to lean outwards owing to the thrust of the roof.

The Charltons of Redesmouth, most famous of the moss-trooper families, have left their mark on local lore and legend that will not easily be forgotten. It was William Charlton of the Bower, generally spoken of as 'Bowrie', who, in 1711, encountered his arch-enemy Henry Widdrington of Buteland, in what turned out to be the last of the sword-fights that took place in the old town. Widdrington was slain in the conflict, and it was ordered that his body should be buried inside the church before Charlton's pew door, on which account, it is said, Bowrie could never again enter Bellingham church.

Episodes of this kind may have little historical importance, but they do reflect the prevailing tense atmosphere of life in North Tynedale long after the old Border forays were already matters of history, so beloved of the poets and ballad-makers.

Bellingham is the last available suitable place for supplies and accommodation, there being few habitations over the next 40 miles/64 km or so. Bellingham youth hostel lies on the outskirts of this ancient border town, and bed and breakfast accommodation is available at the local hotels.

The youth hostel was designed by the late John Dower, and is built in the Norwegian log-cabin style. No meals are provided and there is no store for self-cookers; the general catering position is bad, but there is a snack bar in the town where all meals may be obtained.

Notices in the youth hostel warn of the artillery ranges in Redesdale, but the Pennine Way route follows the boundary of this area for only a short distance. Otterburn Camp should be contacted beforehand, however, if it is intended for some reason to cross the ranges.

It is 15 miles/24 km from Bellingham youth hostel to the youth hostel at Byrness. This later hostel has a small store but does not provide meals, so stock up before you leave Bellingham.

The Tale of the Long Pack

Outside the churchyard are several incised sculptured grave-covers. There is also a mysterious gravestone shaped like a pedlar's pack, with carvings on it as if to represent cords, and engravings of pistols, cutlass and a whistle. Though probably medieval it has been said to be the tomb of the robber who figures in the Ettrick Shepherd's 'Tale of the Long Pack'.

The story runs that in 1723 a Colonel Ridley from India retired to Lee Hall, having acquired a fortune. One winter afternoon while the family was in London a pedlar called at the house and begged a night's lodging. The sole maidservant in charge admitted him, but refused to let him stay; but she did allow him to leave a long and mysterious pack which he said he could carry no farther.

When he had gone the maidservant examined it, and to her horror thought she saw it move. She rushed out for an old farm-hand and he tried to reassure her. Just then the young ploughboy entered, and hearing what had happened, fired at the pack with the gun he used for scaring crows. At once the pack heaved horribly, a great groan came from it, and a wide pool of blood gradually spread over the floor. The ploughboy had killed a robber, and on examination he was found to be armed with four loaded pistols and a cutlass.

The scared servants soon realised that this had been part of a plan for a raid on the house. They hastily set about getting help, and by nightfall 25 armed men were on guard. Nothing happened until one o'clock in the morning when the ploughboy sounded a silver horn he had found on the body. At once it was answered, and soon the sound of galloping hooves was heard.

As the horsemen entered the courtyard they were met with a

volley from the defenders, and they fled, leaving several dead and dying men on the ground. The defenders, fearful of reprisal, dared not venture out; and when day broke it was seen that all the bodies had vanished. Significantly, members of several respectable local families were never seen again in their homes; no-one identified the man in the long-pack, and he was buried in this tomb. So the legend tells.

Bellingham to Redesdale

The Pennine Way from Bellingham now passes beyond the youth hostel on a track via Blakelaw and past Hareshaw House. Do not use the previously defined route to Hareshaw House via Hareshaw Linn, but if you wish to visit this local beauty spot do so by the proper path and retrace your steps to the village. The approach to the Linn is a most delightful walk. Just above the railway the path crosses heaps of shale left behind by the deserted ironworks and skirts a long-neglected dam before the romantic glen reveals itself. The steep and rocky sides of the dene are covered with birches, rowans and ferns, and the rough and narrow pathway leads up and down amongst the trees, crossing and recrossing the stream by wooden bridges.

The lower fall is first reached, a perpendicular ledge of rock 20 ft/6 m high, over which the stream falls in a twin cascade. Half a mile/0·8 km further the main fall of Hareshaw Linn is reached, a shimmering veil of water tumbling over a 60 ft/18 m high ledge which completely seals off the head of the dene, and falling into a gloomy chasm.

With a sudden dash and a bound and splash,
With a rout and shout and roar and din,
The brook, amaz'd, alarm'd and craz'd,
Is sprawling into Hareshaw Linn.
'Tween wooded cliffs, fern-fringed, in falls,
All broken into spray and foam.

J. Clephan

Beyond Hareshaw House the Pennine Way passes west of Abbey Rigg and to the Otterburn road near an old coal mine. Cross the road B6320 and make a line due north to Lough Shaw, 1,102 ft/336 m, and Deer Play, 1,183 ft/361 m. Then cross north-westerly along the line of a parish boundary, passing over Lord's Shaw, 1,167 ft/356 m to a road.

We have now come 7 miles/11·2 km from Bellingham, and

The Linn at the head of Hareshaw Dene

Lough Shaw from the B.6320 north of Bellingham

Byrness Hill

Cottonshopeburn

Blakehopeburnhaugh

Byrness

Prospect through Redesdale Forest

The church and hotel at Byrness

from this point the official route follows a line leading across open country and giving unrivalled views of the Rede valley and the Border and Cheviot hills. The old route past Pit Houses and Gib Shiel is open to motor vehicles and has been relegated in favour of the open moor, but is an alternative in bad weather.

From the road continue north-westerly, keeping a wire fence on your right, past the monument on Padon Hill, 1,240 ft/378 m, and down to a stone wall in the Gib Shiel valley. Turn right through a wicket gate, around the wall corner, back through another wicket gate and continue uphill keeping the stone wall on your right to Brownrigg Head, 1,191 ft/363 m. Turn northwest keeping a wire fence on your right and follow it for a mile/1·6 km to the corner of Redesdale Forest. Cross the fence and continue in the same north-west direction between it and the trees for another ¼-mile/0·4 km to Rookengate, where the road from Gib Shiel enters the forest at height 1,140 ft/347 m.

Redesdale Forest
From the gate the track drops steadily through the forest, and splendid panoramic views open out, extending from Rochester over the northern Cheviots to the Border crossing at Carter Bar. Within 4 miles/6·4 km the track leads to Blakehopeburnhaugh (pronounced 'Blakeupburnhaf') and after crossing a Bailey bridge bears right and crosses a second bridge over the River Rede, and leads to the main Newcastle-Jedburgh road, route A68, ½-mile/0·8 km distant.

Just short of the main road there is a turn left along the line of overhead power cables through fields to Cottonshopeburn Foot. A track crosses to the left of the farm buildings and over the Rede, and we follow this for ½-mile/0·8 km to Raw. A footbridge takes us over the Rede yet again, and the track continues through the Forestry Commission's 'The Raw' picnic area to emerge at the main road by a little stone-tiled church and opposite the Byrness Hotel, a distance of 223 miles/358 km from Edale.

National Park Information Centre and Youth Hostel, Byrness

Byrness

Byrness is one of six villages in the Border Forest Park specially
built to house forestry workers. All designed by Thomas Sharp,
the internationally famous rural and town planner, Byrness was
built in 1951. Not all the houses are occupied now: one is an
information centre for the Northumberland National Park, and
adjoining it are two others which have been converted into a
youth hostel. (The hostel is reached by taking the forestry
track parallel to A68 running westwards from the church.) Other
accommodation in Redesdale is scarce. The Byrness Hotel makes
ramblers welcome with hot baths and good meals, and the petrol
filling station opposite has a cafeteria.

The tiny village church of old Byrness contains a remarkable
window 'in memory of those men, women and children who have
died during the construction of the reservoir at Catcleugh'. The
glass shows workmen labouring with barrow, pick and shovel on
the construction of the reservoir, with an engine and trucks
beside them; and a child sitting on the ground with her father's
dinner in a handkerchief. Above is a medallion portraying a saw,
an axe, and a maul. A thousand men took 15 years to build this
huge reservoir. It has a capacity of 2,305 million gallons/10 478
million litres and supplies Newcastle, 40 miles/64 km away, with
10 million gallons/45 million litres of water daily.

The last stretch of our journey along the Pennine Way involves
27 miles/43 km of very tough going along the highest ridge of the
Cheviots. Almost trackless peat hag and bog, the route must be
covered in one day, unless you expect to use the occasional farms
in Upper Coquetdale for overnight accommodation. However,
magnificent views far into Scotland compensate for the rough
going. Dere Street, The Street and Clennell Street provide
convenient escape routes from the ridge if the weather turns bad
on your last day's march. There are two bad-weather shelters on
the Pennine Way in the Cheviots: one at 1,472 ft/448 m on
Yearning Saddle, SW of Lamb Hill at NGR 805129, and one at
1,631 ft/497 m above Hen Hole at 877202. Neither are to be
relied upon as overnight shelter in winter except in an
emergency—i.e. don't plan beforehand to sleep out in them, but

use them if caught out in bad weather and if you cannot reach
the escape routes.

Redesdale to Lamb Hill

The great green bastions of the Cheviot Hills (pronounced 'Chee-veot') form some of the finest scenery in Northumberland. They also form a natural barrier between England and Scotland, as they extend for about 35 miles/56 km and cover some 200 sq miles/518 sq kms of Northumberland and another 100 sq miles/ 259 sq kms of Roxburghshire.

The steep slopes and uplands of these hills are tenanted by hardy flocks of 'Cheviot' sheep, which retain much of their wild nature. The Cheviots are important sheep country, and two main breeds are to be seen on these hills. The Cheviot breed is kept on the lower land, while the Blackface roam the bleaker heights. The Cheviot is short-wooled, white-faced and hornless, but is best distinguished with its Elizabethan ruff: the Blackface is a horned species with a Roman nose. A more hardy strain than the pure breeds is produced by cross-breeding Cheviot rams with Blackface ewes. The shepherds who live lonely lives in these hills spin their own wool in the winter, and in the summer tend flocks sent from other districts.

Like most hills, the Cheviots have a character all of their own, and to appreciate them it is best to follow the advice of the poet Thomas Pringle, and

> Let our pilgrim footsteps seek
> Old Cheviot's pathless mossy peak;
> For there the Mountain Spirit still
> Lingers round the mountain hill.

Byrness to Chew Green

From the Byrness Hotel to Chew Green is a hill walk of 5 miles/ 8 km. The route takes a forest ride about 200 yds/182 m west of the hotel. Pass some cottages, go through a gate and turn sharp right then left straight up the hillside to the ruins of the fire look-out post on Byrness Hill, 1,358 ft/414 m. This gives a grand view over Redesdale and the Catcleugh Reservoir, with the new Byrness village far away below.

Byrness in Redesdale

Windy Crag   Houx Hill   Saughy Crag   Byrness Hill

Byrness and the Cheviots

The border fence at Coquet Head

Proceeding due north over the open fell it is a simple matter to follow the watershed, which leads over Houx Hill, Windy Crag and Ravens Knowe to Ogre Hill, where a track descends to the Border and Coquet Head.

You now stand at the headwaters of three rivers: southward run tributaries of the Rede towards the Tyne; to the west and north a group of burns wind through Leithope Forest to form the Kale Water which feeds the Tweed; to the east the Coquet begins its meandering course through the Cheviots towards Rothbury. The Tweed basin stretches out to the north-west, while to the north-east the trackless green hills heave like waves of the sea towards the great square mass of the Cheviot, 12 miles/ 19 km distant.

The Border here runs down the course of the Coquet and soon reaches the bold rectangular outlines of the great Roman camps of Chew Green. This route runs just inside the safety zone to the west of a firing range, and is marked with Ministry of Defence posts. This area is not used much, but during the summer months it is unsafe to attempt any return that leads farther EAST.

Redesdale Artillery Range is a vast military training ground, which began as a comparatively circumscribed area near Rochester in Redesdale, but enlarged during the Second World War to take in an enormous tract of country, some 70 sq mls/ 181 sq kms in extent. The range is officially closed to the public when firing is in progress, and this is indicated by the flying of red flags.

Chew Green Roman Camps

Chew Green Camps are sited on a small triangular plateau which formed for the Romans the only suitable camping ground in most difficult country. The camps lie beside the old Roman road of Dere Street which formed the main road into Scotland from the northern military headquarters of York, and are known to have been in use between AD 78 and 185. Temporary camps and permanent forts were crowded into this restricted space until the site became the most complicated and remarkable group of earthworks in the Roman Empire. As the earthworks overlap

Brownhart Law

Dere Street

The Roman Camps of Chew Green from Harden Edge

they are not easy to understand, but they are plainly visible on the bare hillside from the vantage point of Harden Edge.

The biggest is the Great South Camp, covering 22 acres/8·9 ha of the best and driest ground. The Great North Camp covers 15 acres/6 ha, but the best preserved is the West Camp of 6¼ acres/2·5 ha, with notably high and clearly marked ramparts. The South East Fort, about 2 acres/0·8 ha, also has a bold rampart and ditch, while the East Fort has the foundations of a medieval chapel in the middle.

The site must have been an obvious choice as the halting place of the Roman armies marching to the north and as permanent quarters for patrol garrisons, but surrounded by dark hills and monotonous moorland the position of the legionaries in this station must have been one of considerable hardship and discomfort.

The Border: Chew Green to Windy Gyle 6 miles/9·6 km
Dere Street was built by Agricola from York to Scotland, and approaching Chew Green the road becomes known as Gammel's Path, probably from the Danish 'gamel,' meaning old. This was an appointed meeting place of the English and Scottish Lord's Wardens of the Marches for punishing offenders against the Border Laws and settling disputes by single combat; the men of Coquetdale and Redesdale were frequently here for this purpose, and the road was also much used by drovers and smugglers of salt and whisky.

Dere Street and the Pennine Way cross the Coquet stream and turn sharply northwards to run round the shoulder of Brownhart Law, 1,664 ft/507 m, to the Border. On the summit of Brownhart Law, a few yards beyond a wicket gate, is a Roman long-distance signalling-post, from which there is a view of the hills of seven counties.

Twenty-four cairns built with peat sods and topped with temporary notice boards have been erected marking the route of the Pennine Way on the Border; 12 between Brownhart Law and Mozie Law and another 12 between Butt Roads and the Cheviot. Although the Border fence is nonexistent in most parts, the

Mozie Law   Auchope Cairn   Cheviot   Windy Gyle

Buckham's Walls

Prospect of the Cheviots from Brownhart Law

summit ridge is easy to follow except in most severe weather, and then care must be exercised in case the wrong fence is followed, especially in the vicinity of Lamb Hill, Score Head and on Cheviot. Two refuges have been erected for bad weather shelter at 805129 and 877202.

From Brownhart Law the route leads northwards to Black Halls and height 1,464 ft/461 m, then countours round between Broad Flow and Wedder Hill, round the head of Rennies Burn, resuming the Border fence at Lamb Hill 1,677 ft/511 m. Just before this is reached, at NGR 805129, is the first of two bad weather refuges. Then follows Beefstand Hill, 1,842 ft/561 m, and Mozie Law, 1,812 ft/552 m.

Between Mozie Law and Windy Rigg 'The Street' crosses the watershed from the Kale Water to Upper Coquetdale, and if lodging is sought in one of the lonely hill farms then a descent should be made on this track leading south for 3 miles/4·8 km to reach the River Coquet. Carlcroft, Carshope, Rowhope and Trows will be able to provide bed and breakfast provided four weeks notice is given, and only then if out of the sheep-shearing season.

From 'The Street' crossing the Pennine Way leads eastwards over Windy Rigg to Windy Gyle, 2,036 ft/619 m, 8 miles/12·8 km from Chew Green, 13 miles/21 km from Byrness and 14 miles/22·5 km from our destination in Kirk Yetholm. Russell's Cairn is a huge stone tumulus on the summit, said to be the burial place of Sir Francis Russell, who lost his life at Hexpethgate in July 1585 in one of those unfortunate affrays into which the meetings of the Lord's Wardens of the Marches all too frequently developed.

Windy Gyle affords a splendid view of the English side of the hills, while the whole of the Border ridge is in view to the 'stone men' on Auchope Cairn. Half a mile/0·8 km north-east of Windy Gyle we come to another cairn, formerly named Russell's Cairn. Both cairns are probably Bronze Age burial mounds, for the Cheviots are rich in ancient earthworks, hill-forts and homesteads.

Lamb Hill to Kirk Yetholm

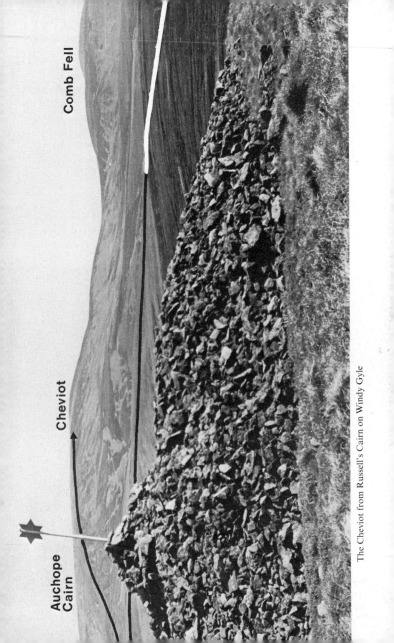

Auchope Cairn

Cheviot

Comb Fell

The Cheviot from Russell's Cairn on Windy Gyle

Windy Gyle to Cheviot 5 miles/8 km

A mile and a half/2·4 km beyond Windy Gyle a gate in the
Border fence marks the crossing of Clennell Street, a grass-grown
track crossing the watershed. Clennell Street is not a Roman
road, as its name might be thought to imply, but a prehistoric
trackway. In the Middle Ages it was known as Hexpethgate at
the Border crossing, and it is now usually called Cocklawgate.
Cock Law, the protruding ridge on the Scottish side, was one of
the recognised places for the meetings of the Lord's Wardens of
the Marches.

In adverse weather conditions it is best to avoid Cheviot, so
descend Clennell Street to Bowmont Water—the easy and safe
way out of troubles—but after Bowmont Water there is a 7 mile/
11·2 km road walk into Kirk Yetholm.

It has been an easy walk down from Windy Gyle, but to follow
the Border towards Cheviot is a much lengthier and laborious
process. Continue on to Butt Roads, 1,718 ft/524 m. King's
Seat, 1,743 ft/531 m, Score Head, 1,910 ft/582 m, and Cairn Hill,
2,545 ft/776 m, where the Pennine Way thrusts out a spur to the
summit of Cheviot, 2,676 ft/815 m, 5 miles/8 km from Windy
Gyle.

The Cheviot

Cheviot can be seen from so many places that it might be
thought to afford wide views, but this is by no means the case.
Daniel Defoe during his grand tour of Scotland in 1726, was
prompted by 'curiosity of no extraordinary kind' to make an
expedition to the summit of what was then practically an
unknown hill. Defoe feared that there might not be room for all
of his party to stand on the top, but there is in fact a flat summit
of some 50 acres/20 ha, and views can be enjoyed only by
walking round the edge of it. To make matters worse the plateau
is covered by an extensive waste of peat hags and bog, so that
steady progress over it is at any time difficult and after heavy
rain is not worth attempting.

Snow generally lies upon Cheviot during half the year, and in
severe winters has been known to remain in the highest ravines

from September to July. Strewn on the heather, bracken and grass slopes lie grey rocks of porphyry, syentie, dolerite and pink granite. Among the coarse wiry grass and bog-mosses grow several mountain plants—the cloudberry or mountain bramble, whose scarlet berries, becoming yellow when they ripen, are scattered over the waste like gems; the red whortle-berry or cow-berry; the crowberry, the bilberry, cotton grass, cow wheat, rigid carex and three species of clubmoss.

A heap of stones called the Western Cairn is the highest point, and not far away is a deep crater filled to the rim with water. This marks the scene of a tragedy, when in December, 1944, a Flying Fortress of the USAAF laden with bombs on its way to Germany, crashed during a late afternoon blizzard. The two shepherds who saved the seven crew—two were killed in the crash—received the British Empire Medal; and their sheepdog that found them became the first animal, other than one actually serving with the armed or civil defence forces, to receive the Dickin Medal—the animals' Victoria Cross.

The view from the plateau ridge is most extensive—north to the Lammermuir Hills of Scotland beyond the Tweed, west to the 'three peaked Eildons', south to the uplands of Durham, and east to the coast and the Farne Islands, Holy Island and Coquet Island standing out from the blue, green and grey waters. South-west is the prospect of the long line of the conical, grass-covered summits of the Cheviot range.

Cheviot to Auchope Cairn 2 miles/3·2 km

From Cheviot summit return to Cairn Hill and the Border fence, at a height of 2,300 ft/701 m passing the Hanging Stone, a rock which derives its name from the circumstance of a packman being strangled by his pack slipping over the edge and tightening the strap around his neck. This fractured rocky outcrop, 17 ft/5 m high, is now 200 yds/182 m inside England, though in medieval times was actually on the Border, and in addition formed the boundary of the Eastern and Middle Marches.

Half a mile/0·8 km north-west is Auchope Cairn, 2,382 ft/ 726 m, a prominent peak on the Border, distinguished by several

Auchope Cairn from height 2,419 ft near Cairn Hill

The Schil ►

Hen Hole

Prospect into Scotland from Auchope Cairn

Burnhead Farm and the Halterburn Valley

large cairns on the crest of its narrow ridge. It has one of the widest views in Britain, and with binoculars it is possible to see the mountain Lochnager by Balmoral, well over 100 miles/ 160 km away in the Highlands.

The Hen Hole

To the north of Auchope Cairn is the chasm of Hen Hole, so deep and so narrow that the sun never enters it, and often holding a small patch of snow even at midsummer. Black cliffs rise steeply to a height of 250 ft/76 m on either side of this lonely and lovely ravine, where raven and peregrine falcon nest on inaccessible ledges. From the summit of Cheviot a peaty burn splashes down from ledge to ledge forming pretty waterfalls, fringed with ferns and mosses, and issuing from the dreadful gorge of the College Burn.

The Hen Hole is a famous hunting ground for the botanist, who will find in its rock recesses or the vicinity the star saxifrage, the cut-leaved or mossy saxifrage, alpine sowthistle, chickweed epilobe, the rare dwarf cornel, green spleenwort, teeth fern, curled or parsley fern, floating sweet grass or Balfour's pea, serrated winter green and black willow.

Foxes are occasionally hunted into the Hole, and there is a tradition of a party of huntsmen being lured into the chasm by the sweetest music they had ever heard, and could never again find their way out. Apart from being the haunt of fairies, local legend asserts that this gloomy gorge was the hiding place of Black Adam of Cheviot, one of the most notorious of Borderland freebooters, who murdered the bride of Wight Fletcher at Wooperton. Scott, in his 'Minstrelsy of the Scottish Border', tells the ballad of Black Adam bursting in upon a wedding party when the bridegroom was away to fetch the priest, robbing the women guests of their jewels and ravishing and killing the bride. On his return Fletcher tracked the murderer to the Hen Hole, but Black Adam escaped the bridegroom by a desperate leap of seven yards or more into his lair, a cave in the side of the steep cliff.

The Village Green at Kirk Yetholm, and the end of the Pennine Way

Descent to Kirk Yetholm

From Auchope Cairn the Border fence is followed westerly over Auchope Rigg then northerly to the Schil, 1,985 ft/605 m, a prominent cone with distinctive rocks around its summit, possibly a Bronze Age burial cairn.

The fence leads down to a path at the head of Fleehope Burn, and this path is followed north-west round Black Hag, leaving the Border and descending to Burnhead and the Halterburn valley.

The hills are now behind us. A metalled road takes us round the foot of Staerough Hill to Kirk Yetholm, and the end of our 250 mile/402 km Pennine Way journey.

Kirk Yetholm is a place of some antiquity, and was once the 'capital' of the notorious gipsy clan of the Faas that once flourished in the Border. A row of houses across the green from the pleasant, thatch-roofed Border Hotel is still called Gipsy Row, and a small cottage above this with an ivy-fronted porch was known as the Gipsy Palace. Kirk Yetholm had an evil reputation in those days, but the 'dynasty' declined, and the last 'queen', Esther Fall (or Faa) Blyth, was buried in the churchyard in 1835.

It has been a long stretch of 27 miles/43 km without shelter from Byrness, but Kirk Yetholm can provide accommodation at the Hartleyburn Private Hotel or the Scottish Youth Hostel. The hostel is well equipped for self cookers though no meals are provided, and enquiries from the warden will direct you to a cottage where good meals will be provided, including an early breakfast so as to enable you to catch the early bus to Kelso. Kelso is the nearest town of any size with public transport to take you back home in comfort.

On the Pennine Way you have enjoyed magnificent scenery, with wooded valleys, barren moorlands, tumbling waterfalls, Roman roads and old bridleways, wild life but above all the get-away-from-it-all feeling that only the hills can give. If you were not fit at the start you should be now, and if you have the time and the determination you will turn around and walk the length of the Pennine Way again, southwards to Edale where you started.

Weary with toil, I haste me to my bed,
The dear repose for limbs with travel tir'd;
But then begins a journey in my head,
To work my mind, when body's work's expir'd.

William Shakespeare

Title	Author	Publisher
The Pennine Way	K. Oldham	Dalesman 1960
Walking the Pennine Way	A. P. Binns	Gerrard 1966
The Pennine Way in 20 days	H. O. Wade	Harold Hill 1966
The Shell Book of the Pennine Way	M. Marriott	Queen Anne Press 1968
Pennine Way Companion	A. Wainwright	Westmorland Gazette 1968
The Pennine Way	T. Stephenson	HMSO 1969
Along the Pennine Way	J. H. B. Peel	Cassell 1969
A Walker on The Pennine Way	C. Walker	Pendyke Publications 1974
Mountain Trail	J. Wood	Allen & Unwin 1947
Peak Panorama	W. A. Poucher	Chapman & Hall 1946
Backbone of England	W. A. Poucher	Country Life 1946
Peak & Pennines	W. A. Poucher	Constable 1966
High Peak	E. Byne & G. J. Sutton	Secker & Warburgh 1966
Buildings of England	N. Pevsner	Penguin 1959
Scenery of England & Wales	A. E. Trueman	Gollancz 1938
Wild Flowers of Chalk & Limestone	J. F. Lousley	Collins 1950
Wanderings in the Pennines	W. T. Palmer	Skeffington 1951
The Kings England Series	A. Mee	Hodder & Stoughton 1936–52
Peak District National Park		HMSO 1960
The Peak District	K. C. Edwards	Collins 1962
Lancashire & the Pennines	F. Singleton	Batsford 1952
The Roof of Lancashire	H. C. Collins	Dent 1950
Striding Through Yorkshire	A. J. Brown	Country Life 1949
Yorkshire & the North East	A. Raistrick	Oliver & Boyd 1963
Comprehensive Guide to Northumberland	W. W. Tomlinson	W. Scott 1935
Border National Forest Park		HMSO 1958
Guide to the Cheviot Hills	F. R. Banks	Reid 1950
Scottish Border Country	F. R. Banks	Batsford 1951
Handbook of the Roman Wall	C. Bruce	Reid 1957